Vocation

SETTING FOR
HUMAN FLOURISHING

Vocation

THE SETTING FOR HUMAN FLOURISHING

FOREWORD BY
RALEIGH SADLER

MICHAEL BERG

Vocation: The Setting for Human Flourishing

© 2020 New Reformation Publications

Scriptures taken from the Holy Bible, New International Version®, NIV®. Copyright © 1973, 1978, 1984, 2011 by Biblica, Inc.™ Used by permission of Zondervan. All rights reserved worldwide. www.zondervan.com The "NIV" and "New International Version" are trademarks registered in the United States Patent and Trademark Office by Biblica, Inc.™

Published by:
1517 Publishing
PO Box 54032
Irvine, CA 92619-4032

Publisher's Cataloging-In-Publication Data
(Prepared by The Donohue Group, Inc.)

Names: Berg, Mike, 1978– author. | Sadler, Raleigh, writer of supplementary textual content.
Title: Vocation : the setting for human flourishing / by Michael Berg ; foreword by Raleigh Sadler.
Description: Irvine, CA : 1517 Publishing, [2021] | Includes bibliographical references.
Identifiers: ISBN 9781945978982 (hardcover) | ISBN 9781945978999 (paperback) | ISBN 9781948969307 (ebook)
Subjects: LCSH: Vocation (in religious orders, congregations, etc.) | Christian life. | Righteousness.
Classification: LCC BX2380 .B47 2021 (print) | LCC BX2380 (ebook) | DDC 253.2—dc23

Printed in the United States of America

Cover art by Brenton Clarke Little

Contents

Foreword

"God, why won't you save me?" I have prayed these words like a mantra. Each time, I hoped my fear would give way to a newfound sense of freedom. However, the more I prayed, the more exhausted I became.

For as long as I can remember, I've sought God's approval over everything else. If the doors of the church were open, I was there. If I wasn't at church, you could rest assured that I was praying or attempting to read my Bible. This is what a "good Christian" is supposed to do, right?

I wanted to be a good Christian more than anything— but therein lay the problem. I was focusing more on what I was doing than what Christ had done for me on the cross. Without knowing it, I was hopelessly and desperately trying to secure my vertical relationship with God.

This insidious desire to prove myself followed me to seminary. With each completed assignment, I white-knuckled my way toward eternal security, believing that though we are saved by grace through faith, I still needed to do something to experience the freedom I had been promised.

The freedom came, but it was not based on anything I had done. As was usual, I waited until the last minute to write a paper for my Introduction to Church History class. Much to my dismay, the shelves of the library had been picked clean. Given that I had few options left at this point,

I grabbed the only two books still available. The more I read, the more my eyes were opened to the finished work of Christ. To be honest, freedom never came through introspection for me. It came only as I looked away from myself to the finished work of Christ.

Upon realizing that the question of whether or not God loved me had been answered over two thousand years ago, I was now free to love others. As Gustaf Wingren famously put it in *Luther on Vocation*, "God doesn't need your good works, but your neighbor does." In other words, God's grace empowers us to love our neighbors through what we do daily. The righteousness of Christ frees us from being curved inward and propels us outward toward our neighbor in vocation. In my case, it led me to start Let My People Go, an organization that exists to mobilize the local church to fight human trafficking by loving those most vulnerable.

Michael Berg's *Vocation: The Setting for Human Flourishing* reminds us that God doesn't love you any more or any less based on your vocational choices. Instead, your vocation is how God chooses to love people through you. We don't need to have the perfect or most fulfilling job to change the world. As Berg says, "The ditch digger is just as important as the priest." While one vocation is no better than another, each of us can impact others as we serve them through our vocations. *Vocation* is a refreshing reminder of this essential truth.

—Raleigh Sadler
Author of *Vulnerable:
Rethinking Human Trafficking*

Introduction

Two Lessons Learned

A Lesson in Vocation

> It is in the nature of the human being to seek a justification for his actions.
> —Aleksandr Solzhenitsyn, *The Gulag Archipelago*

As a young pastor, I was a fish out of water. I was a city kid sent to a rural town of 430 to pastor a church of 360. Wood Lake, Minnesota, was the last place I imagined myself, but the Holy Spirit made me a fool. The twelve years I lived in that farming community will be, when all is said and done, some of the best years of my life. The people were good to me—better than I deserved. It wasn't just the way they loved my family and me or dutifully listened to my early (and subpar) sermons with patient ears. It was because they taught me as much as I taught them. I tried very hard, especially early on, not to be a burden. I am a pastor's kid, so I know the drill. It's a privilege to serve. The church comes first. When the parsonage needs new carpet and the church needs new windows, we'll make sure the church gets new windows by not even bringing up the fact that we are literally sewing two pieces of carpet together in the hallway in our home (that last part is a true story from my childhood). I am fine with that.

About three years into this preaching gig, we had a financial scare. The congregation was low on funds, not because of low offerings, but because of health insurance. Premiums had quickly and dramatically risen, placing all companies in a precarious position, especially nonprofits. I was sitting on a cold metal chair in a church basement before twenty or so hardworking, no-nonsense farmers who never saw an expenditure they couldn't scrutinize (in their own budget, the church's budget, and of course, the government's budget). We had to discuss health insurance. Should we continue with the church-sponsored insurance with high premiums but good coverage, or should we find a different company and take on the risk of higher deductibles? This same question was being asked in lowly church basements and high-powered board rooms across the country.

After everyone had their say and the awkwardness of people talking about your compensation *in front of you* wore off, I decided to speak. Pastor-speak. Leader-speak. Pious-speak. I declared that my family would be OK with the higher deductible. A hand went up. The chairman of the congregation, a retired farmer with a John Wayne drawl and a cowboy hat to match, called on the man: "But we don't want to put the pastor into a bad situation if one of his kids gets sick. The liability is not worth the risk."

Before our chairman, who was sitting next to me, could call for more discussion, I swooped in with glorious piety: "God will take care of my family and me."

After hearing my attempt at virtue, our chairman, Jerome Timm, chuckled. He put his right hand on my shoulder and said, "Pastor, *we* are how God takes care of you." He called for a vote. It was unanimous. They would pay for the better insurance. This is how God would take care of me: through this congregation. I had been taught a lesson in vocation that night.

A Lesson in Justification

I was also taught a lesson in justification. As I walked the one block to my home that evening, I thought to myself, "To hell with my piety." Who was I trying to impress? These men? Myself? God? My self-justification tried to get in the way of a gift. God used these people to feed my family (figuratively and literally—we got the best beef and pork we'll ever eat—and some chicken too). This was a gift. Why would I turn down a gift from God? How insulting to the giver! It was worse than that. I tried to replace the gift with a work. It was a form of self-justification. My motives were half pure. I truly wanted the best financial outcome for the church, but I also wanted to be seen as valuable, worthy, and unselfish. I wanted to be righteous. I wanted to justify my existence and value to my congregation. I tried to turn down God's gift in order to make myself *look* righteous. God's gift in exchange for my work. To hell with my piety.

Vocation and justification collided in my mind that evening when Mr. Timm said, "*We* are how God takes care of you." Justification is a big theological word, but we all understand its ordinary meaning. If I come home from work today pulling a fifty-thousand-dollar speedboat behind my vehicle, I need to *justify* that purchase to my wife. I need to make my actions look right—that is, just. I need to justify my actions. I need to justify myself. We do this all the time. I think it is why we make sure to let people around us know that we pull our own weight. "I did the dishes," I say to my wife, subtly letting her know that I am a good husband (and that I am keeping a mental tally of the housework). I am justifying my value (myself) by my actions. This is a dead end with God. What could I do that would impress him? Not to mention the long list of tasks left undone, done poorly, or, as in the case of all my deeds, done with impure motives. I cannot justify myself before God, but here is the good news: I don't have to. Christ justifies me. He makes me right. His righteousness becomes my righteousness, and my sin becomes his sin. He marches to the cross with my sin, and I am presented before God with his righteousness (2 Cor. 5:21; Rom. 3:21–26).

These two lessons, one in vocation and one in justification, cannot be separated. First, vocation, or calling, assumes a caller (God) and the called (the Christian). There must be a relationship between God and the person; vocation is exclusive to justified believers.[1] Second, vocation assumes freedom from the burden of pleasing God. If the Christian's time and energy are exhausted in an attempt to earn favor with God, there is nothing left for the neighbor. It is true that vocation is in the realm of law. It is how God uses Christians to love the world. My work in vocation is not how I am saved. Vocation is not gospel.[2] Vocation is not for heaven. Yet vocation is only possible because heaven is secure. Only the justified *in* Christ can work *with* Christ in the Father's economy of love. I was free as a young pastor to receive from God through my people. There was no need to justify myself. I was free. I was free to love.

With heaven secure and my livelihood in good hands (God's hands), I looked up and saw my neighbor. I was set free to lose myself in the craft of my vocation. I was free to love both my job and my people. I was freed from the worries that debilitate us so often: finances, life-work balance, job performance—all the stresses of the world. God would get his work done with or without me. For every task I perform in my many callings, there is an untold number of people God uses in their callings to love me. The work will get done. I did not need to be the hero with bad health insurance. And the funny thing about that confidence in

God was that it didn't make me lazy; it actually made me more productive. The pressure was off.

Don't get me wrong. I was, and am, a mess—a sinner-saint.[3] I am always, in some way, working against God and sinning against the callings in which he has placed me. Vocation is where I do spiritual battle. Vocation is the ring in which the old Adam and the new creation spar. This is where I suffer. This is where I bear a cross. This shouldn't surprise me, for I am Christ's coworker. He puts me on as his mask to love my wife, my children, and all the people with whom I interact. This is really about Christ loving my neighbors, and I just happen to be a part of the equation. I decrease so that he might increase. Should I not share in his sufferings? Will there not be a cross? When I live for them, I die to myself. This is a spiritual battle.

Yet the burden is light. Once again, for every vocation I fill, there are countless vocations through which God loves me. I receive much more than I give. I receive my daily bread through a myriad of people carrying out their vocations. I am gifted the elements of human flourishing such as freedom, prosperity, and security. I am taught respect for human beings because now I see my neighbors as Christ working for me through them. Through my own vocations, I am given purpose and true self-esteem. I am blessed with proper honor and pride in my work. I am given a reason to get up in the morning. I am once again taught the value of a human being, for when I serve my neighbor, I serve Christ.

A Call to Serve Our Neighbor

This is ultimately what vocation is about: God serves our neighbors through us as we carry out our vocations. As I alluded to above, *vocation* means "calling." Everybody has a station in life—multiple stations, in fact. A woman may be a mother, lawyer, aunt, citizen, wife, volunteer at a local school, and so on. This is where she *stands*. These are her stations. Notice that these are all God-approved. If this woman also happens to be a loan shark, that is not a station. It is a false station masquerading as a real position in God's ordered creation. Proper stations take on new meaning for the Christian. The Christian is called by God to perform acts of love in those stations. They are more than stations; they are vocations or callings.

It is difficult to differentiate between station and vocation. The atheist lawyer may outperform his Christian colleague. That's not the point. The first difference is justification, which frees the Christian to love. The second difference is the concept of the neighbor. Through the lens of vocation, the neighbor looks different. The neighbor is the goal of the vocational action. It is a divine transaction: God's love through vocation to the neighbor. So who is my neighbor? It's not as easy a question as we might think (Luke 10:29). The answer is everybody with whom you interact. If you are a wife, then your neighbor is your husband. If you are a father, then your kids are your neighbors. If you are a nurse, your patients, coworkers, and employers are your neighbors. If you are the CEO of a large company, then your employees, clients, vendors, stockholders, and the government you pay taxes to are your neighbors. If your company has a large enough economic and environmental reach, then everybody is your neighbor. Finally, your neighbor is the person God serves through you.

We also want to be careful about our definitions of *calling*. There are different commands and invitations from God that can be characterized as "callings." It is necessary to distinguish vocation from other callings to avoid mixing law with gospel or sanctification (the holy life Christians live) with justification. Christ's call to faith is a gospel matter—sinners are declared righteous through faith. The call to work is a law matter—the righteous are made to love their neighbors. The term *call* is used in the New Testament in reference to both the call to trust God (2 Thess. 2:14) and the call to a holy life (2 Tim. 1:9). Peter used the word to describe a call into a life that will include suffering (1 Pet. 2:21). The term is also used to refer to a call into the apostolic ministry (Rom. 1:1) or any station in life (1 Cor. 7:20).

In summary, the term *call* in the New Testament can refer to the call to faith, a call to a sanctified life, a call to suffer, a call to a specific action, a call to a particular office, and a call to a station in life. Each one is related. The call to faith leads to a holy life, which includes suffering. This sanctified life is directed by God's commands of specific actions that may entail specific offices or stations in life (e.g., mother, doctor, pastor) or, in the case of converts, a new perspective and purpose in the stations in which they already find themselves.

The most important call is the call to faith. Without a call to faith, the sinner remains in his iniquity (John 3:18). Without a call to faith, work lacks spiritual meaning (Heb. 11:6). The call to faith is a matter of justification. Those who believe are crucified with Christ and resurrected into a new life (Rom. 6:1–4). Those newly alive in Christ are also called to a sanctified life, as St. Paul wrote in his introduction to his first letter to the Corinthians: "To the church of God in Corinth, to those sanctified in Christ Jesus and called to be his holy people" (1 Cor. 1:2).

This raises the question, "How do we know when God is calling?" At times, God spoke directly to his chosen people to perform specific sanctified deeds. He called Noah to build an ark (Gen. 6:13–14) and called Peter to accept Gentiles into the church (Acts 10:9–22). Yet for most believers, God will never speak to them directly but rather through his Word as preached and written. Still, he is intimately involved in their lives. He calls them too. This is the call to a specific vocation.

For example, when God gives the gift of life and offers guidelines for mothers (Prov. 31:10–31), he calls a woman to the vocation of mother. When God demands that business be conducted fairly (Lev. 19:13), he calls the businessman into a vocational relationship with his customers, employees, the government, stockholders, and the community in which he conducts business.

Vocation as the Setting for Human Flourishing

One way to think about vocation is to perceive it as a setting—that is, the place or situation in which certain actions occur. Vocation is the setting for God's work in the world, spiritual warfare, and ultimately human flourishing.

Vocation is the setting for God's work in the world. This is his economy of love. It's how he gets things done. He uses the ordinary to accomplish the extraordinary in a complex but beautifully simple web of neighborly interactions. God could easily have dinner prepared for you when you return home from work: a beautiful spread of comfort food laid out on a red and white checkered tablecloth draping a picnic table in your beautiful backyard. He's done it before. He fed the Israelites this way for forty years (Exod. 16:35). He doesn't do that anymore today, but he still feeds us. Now he uses the farmer, the truck driver, the grocer, the FDA inspector, the person who prepares the meal, and others. He uses them to feed you. He works through people.

Vocation is also the setting for spiritual warfare. Here the Christian does battle with the devil. In each vocation, the Christian is called to die to self and to live for others. The devil continually attempts to thwart such love. He will attack God's order by mixing up vocations. He will attack the individual with thoughts of improper pride and self-justification. He tries to turn vocation from a calling to serve into an avenue of self-justification.

Finally, vocation is the setting for human flourishing. God provides us with *purpose*, *freedom*, *security*, and *prosperity* through vocations. These four components allow for humanity to flourish. The tragedy of a sinful world is evident in the lack of flourishing. Human flourishing is the way it is supposed to be (and will be in heaven). Sin is the opposite, the way it is not supposed to be. Each vocation works toward this flourishing. In this way, individuals are given divine and grand purposes beyond their survival or success.

None of this works or even matters without peace in Christ. Christ must free us from work so that we can work. Freedom from the unbearable burden of pleasing God is the freedom to be who we were always intended to be: people of love. We cannot separate vocation from justification. You need the former to carry out the latter properly. As Martin Luther paraphrased Paul, "A Christian is a perfectly free lord of all, subject to none. A Christian is a perfectly dutiful servant to all, subject to all."[4]

I learned two lessons that night in the church basement: one in vocation, the other in justification. God would take care of me through other people and their vocations. This is a gift. My attempt to deny the gift for some sort of piety was insane. To hell with my piety. I am free from that self-imposed law. I am free to love.

Chapter 1

Freed to Love

Human Potential

We tend to assume that the Bible here is using human institutions and relationships—marriage, fatherhood—as figures of speech to help us understand something about God and spiritual reality. The human relationships are the primary reality, which can help us understand by analogy, certain spiritual truths. The doctrine of vocation, however, encourages us to reverse the analogy. The primary reality is in God. Our Father in heaven is the true father, of which earthly fathers are pale reflections. Christ is the true son. Christ's relationship with the church is the true marriage. It isn't like Christ is like a bridegroom; he is the bridegroom. Earthly bridegrooms are like Christ. The spiritual realities can help us understand something about human relationships.

—Gene Edward Veith and Mary Moerbre,
Family Vocation

My father never told me that he was proud of me. I am sure he did; I just don't remember it. To be honest, I didn't do much to earn those words. I was a lazy student, a subpar athlete, and an awful musician. There wasn't much I accomplished that would inspire my father to point and declare, "That's *my* boy!" Of course, as typical of American males, he didn't have to say it anyway. Some things are just understood. But I don't think that's the reason he never said it (or that I don't remember it). He didn't say it because it would have been weird. Only in certain circumstances would you say that you are proud of an equal, like your spouse or a friend. You may be proud *to know* someone who has accomplished something great, but you are not proud *of* him or her. I wouldn't approach a colleague, pat him on the head, and say, "Proud of you, buddy!" It would be more than weird; it would be demeaning. As if he was looking for my approval in the first place.

Whether he did it consciously or not, I think this was why my father never said that he was proud of me. He treated me as an equal. He respected me. He respected me before I earned it or deserved it. We are both pastors (now I teach at a college), so we have a lot in common. When we talked theology when I was younger, he never berated me or belittled me for saying something stupid or even wrong, even though I did. He respected me as an intellectual equal far before I was. It would have been weird for him to say "Proud of you, buddy" to an equal. So he never did. Or, probably more accurately, I don't remember him saying it because it didn't matter to me. He had already shown me respect even though I didn't deserve it.

Perhaps there is an insight into the Father in heaven, of whom my father and all fathers are a picture. Can we say that God respects us? Considering that he makes us his coworkers in vocation, I think he does on some level. We are certainly not his equals. Before the fall into sin, Adam and

Eve would have never claimed equality with God. In fact, the desire to be like him was the impetus of their fall into sin. At the same time, we are created in the image of God. This is deserving of respect and rights as well. Even better, he redeemed us and treats us like sons who inherit the family estate (Gal. 3:26–28).[1] This is pure grace because we most certainly do not deserve this love or respect.

I am fascinated with the Tower of Babel account in Genesis. God respects human potential even though he has the power to squash any human endeavor. After seeing the people of earth building a tower to reach into the heavens, God said, "Nothing will be impossible for them." An exaggeration for sure, but the respect God has for the potential of humanity fascinates me. It was almost as if God was scared of his creation: "If as one people speaking the same language they have begun to do this, then nothing they plan to do will be impossible for them. Come, let us go down and confuse their language so they will not understand each other" (Gen. 11:6–7).

Human potential is extraordinary. This potential is finite, certainly, for we are finite creatures. Yet the ceiling is higher than we can perceive. From our point of view, our potential seems infinite. This is terrifying. The potential for evil I possess is chilling. It was not the tyrants who carried out the infamous genocides of our history; it was regular people who did the dirty work. Ordinary people like me. We are fools to underestimate our potential for evil. The opposite is true as well. It is true that our potential for good is limited by our finitude and is severely hampered by our sinfulness.[2] Still, we underestimate the potential of God to work good through us.

I experienced this when my wife was pregnant with our first child. As the eldest of six children, I knew what was coming when it came time for me to be a parent. I was not the young father who didn't know how to hold an infant or change a diaper. Nothing surprised me as a new parent. This did not make me, however, a confident new parent. I was terrified because I knew what kind of patience and love it would take, and I didn't have it. I thought I had a ceiling for love, and that limit had been met. Then I held that baby girl in my arms for the first time, and my ceiling was shattered. I had a greater potential for love than I thought. When my wife was pregnant with our second child, I literally thought I wouldn't love the second child. How could I? I couldn't take one ounce of love away from my first child—I was tapped out. Then I held that second baby girl in my arms. My ceiling was shattered again. By the time the third baby girl came along, I knew what would happen. I could have a dozen children, and I would have enough love for them all. I wouldn't have the time, energy, patience, or money for all of them, but I would have the love (as sinfully watered down as that love might be).

This tremendous human potential originates from God. We who are created in the image of God are very different from the lifeless rock. We move on our own. We possess this mysterious thing called life. We are different from plants—we have consciousness—we can think and love and play. We are different from animals that think, play, and maybe even love. We are made in the image of God with all the beauty, complexity, and rationality that comes along with this divine imprint. We have lost original righteousness; that is, we have lost the perfect image of God, but there remains something about us that separates us from all the rest of creation. We have wonderment. We were made for greatness. Above all, we are loved by the creator so much that he desires to redeem us. We are ones for whom Christ died. We are justifiable in the sense that God justifies us and not the rocks.

There is an innate value we possess. We instinctively know that we were made for something great, certainly greater than this fallen world. We generally see someone who does not live up to their potential as tragic and not admirable. "What a waste," we might comment. There is a desire for perfection, a desire for heaven, a desire for wholeness. We are told to be content and rightly so (1 Tim. 6:6), and yet how could we ever be content? How could we ever settle for a life that ends in death? We were made for life, not death. We should never settle for mediocrity. Our discontent is sinful (everything we do is), but it is also righteous. It is part and parcel of being simultaneously a sinner-saint. The sinner is discontent and selfishly whines, but the saint is discontent with eager anticipation of what is to come (Gal. 5:5). Either way, we are people of drama. We know there is more. I am convinced that if we don't have drama in our lives, we will make it up. Such is our innate desire for greatness.

We tend to put drama in the wrong place, which hampers our freedom. We get worked up about unimportant matters and are flippant about important ones. We free ourselves where we should be bound and imprison ourselves where we are free. I am perplexed by Hollywood stars. On the one hand, they hate the paparazzi. I understand. Who wants their whole life plastered across cheap magazines or trashy websites? Yet, nothing promotes itself like Hollywood. There seems to be an endless parade of award shows. "Another one?" I think to myself as I hear about the red carpet at the Oscars, Golden Globes, Emmy's, and so on and so forth. My immediate self-righteousness criticizes the whole spectacle: "What a bunch of self-absorbed narcissists!" But perhaps there is a tragic lesson for us all. We will never be satisfied. Part of that is sinful pride (sinner), but a part of this is truly righteous discontent (saint). I was made for perfection, and nothing this side of perfection will ever satisfy. Nothing. The sinful self will never be satisfied, but neither will the saint created in the image of God. The sinner is bound to other's praise. It's another form of self-justification. When we seek drama, importance, and value in the wrong places, freedom is hampered. We strive for validation and not flourishing. The saint is never satisfied either, not because she is seeking justification but rather a world that flourishes—the way it was always intended to be.

We should talk about freedom for a moment. At first glance, it seems that freedom should be defined as "To do whatever I want, whenever I want, however I want, and as often as I want." But is this true freedom? The addict says the same thing: "It's my body and my life. I can do what I want." We all understand that this is not freedom but the worst kind of prison, one of his own making. I am no freer than the addict when I sin. I am a slave to sin (Rom. 6, 7). My "freedom" to do what I want is no freedom at all. It's the worst kind of prison.

Freedom is found in Christ. First, I know that I do not need to work for the approval of the Father. In Christ, I am made righteous. I can't please God, and I don't have to. Christ already did that for me. I am free from the burdensome question, "Am I good enough for God?" The answer is no, but Christ makes it yes (2 Cor. 1:19–20). Second, I am free from finding justification for my existence and value from the world. A created-in-the-image-of-God human is never going to be satisfied with such accolades anyway. And what could ever be greater than being made one in Christ? A promotion, an award, a raise, a Noble Peace Prize, an Emmy, an Oscar? I am free from finding value in all the wrong places because I have value in Christ.

The builders of the Tower of Babel were never going to reach the heavens. How could they? The height of the building was not what concerned God; it was the desire to do so in the first place. The builders of the tower wanted to make a name for themselves. Why? Who were they trying to impress? Themselves? God? Since they were created in the image of God, they had an inborn desire for greatness. What could be greater than reaching into the heavens? What could be greater than to play God? The irony is that our desire to be like God is what gets us into trouble. We only make matters worse. The tragedy is that God actually provides divine deeds for us to accomplish. We have it upside down. We consider making a name for ourselves a thing of glory, but the glory is never attained. Christ tells us differently. His glory is in the cross—no red carpet for him. Our glory is first in the cross as well. Here is where our sins are forgiven, and we are made righteous. Second are our lives of serving others in vocation. God prepares divine works in advance for us to accomplish (Eph. 2:10). To be like God is not to make a name for ourselves; it is to love.

Humanity has not stopped building towers of Babel despite the confusion of our languages. List your towers of Babel. Maybe it is a perfect house or a perfect family. Perhaps a high-paying job, fancy letters behind your name, or a corner office. The problem is that there is always one more story that can be built upon the tower. Another promotion, one more zero on the end of the paycheck, one more championship, one more accolade. I could win thirty Nobel Peace prizes and would still want one more. It's a prison of the worst kind because we made it for ourselves. If we would only stop trying to make a name for ourselves and look around, we would see great and glorious tasks laid at our feet. They would just appear differently. They would look like crosses.

Two Kinds of Righteousness

From this you will see that monasticizing and making spiritual regulations is all wrong in our time. For these people bind themselves before God to outward things from which God has made them free thus working against the freedom of faith and God's order. On the

> other hand, where these people should be bound,
> namely, in their relations with other men and in serv-
> ing every man in love, there they make themselves
> free, serving no one and being of no use to anyone but
> themselves, thus working against love.
>
> —Martin Luther

I have never been able to shake this desire for self-justification, and I won't this side of heaven. This desire for self-justification plays out in my life every single day, even in the simplest of situations. When I drive to work in the morning and find myself behind a slow driver, I think to myself, "Must be nice to take a leisurely Sunday drive, but it's *Tuesday* morning, and I have places to be!" What I am really saying is, "Don't these people know how important I am?" On the way home from work, I notice a driver tailgating me. Now I think, "Slow down, buddy. What's the rush? I have places to be too." What I am really saying is, "I am just as important as you." In each situation, I attempt to justify my worth. But to whom am I justifying myself? Am I trying to justify my value to another driver who can't even hear my inner monologue? Am I trying to justify myself to myself? Am I God? Even within myself, all alone in a car, I am still trying to find value for myself. I end up playing God like the Babel architects. It's the ultimate idolatry. It is God alone who justifies, not me.

Maybe it is guilt that pushes me into this insanity. I should have accomplished more by now. I should be the one with important places to be. So I overcompensate by convincing myself that if I don't arrive at my destination soon, everything will fall apart. I am so important. Maybe it is competitiveness. "You're not better than me. I am just as important as you," I say to imaginary critics. Either way, I am trying to raise my profile while lowering the profile of someone else—someone that I will never meet in the example above.

I am willing to bet that you put yourself under impossible laws all the time too. Always in a competition. Always judging others not necessarily because you care so much about them but because you care so much about yourself. You attempt to decrease others so that you might increase yourself—a reversal of John the Baptist's famous line (John 3:30). I am willing to bet that it does not end well for you either. It accomplishes nothing in the end but bitterness toward an unfair system or self-pity: "I have it so rough, rougher than anybody else."

This is all a symptom of a theological misunderstanding. St. Paul tells us that there are two kinds of righteousness. We might think of them as two systems. The first is a righteousness by law, and the second is a righteousness by faith. In system one, we build righteous towers of Babel. In system two, we do nothing. In the first system, righteousness is earned. A person follows laws and is rewarded. In the second system, righteousness is given. Christ is righteous, and his righteousness is given to the sinner. The sinner believes, and it is credited to him as righteousness (Gen. 15:6). If we put ourselves into the first system, we are asking God to judge us by our deeds according to the law. This is a victory for the devil. He loves to play the prosecutor who says to the judge (God), "These are your laws, and this person has not kept them. You must punish him." In the second system, our lawyer (Christ) says, "Take my righteous life and credit it to my client." Refusing the advocate's advice is akin to being your own lawyer: "I can make a case for my life."[3] And you know what they say about a person who serves as his own lawyer: "He has a fool for a client."

The first system, a righteousness by law, is generally how the world works. This is a good thing. People are (usually) judged by what they do. There are rules (law), and those who follow the rules do well. Those who break the rules do not. This is, however, a terrible system for love. Love becomes an earned wage and not a gift. It is no longer love; it is an obligation. God no longer loves us but is obligated to pay us the correct wage for our actions. He is no longer Father to us but rather a business partner—and a merciless one at that. How could a sinner ever do well in a system like this?

The second system, a righteousness by faith, is how God deals with his people. This is a very good thing. People are not judged by what they do. There are rules (law), but they are not what makes a person righteous (how could a sinner ever do that?). Instead, Christ is righteous in the sinner's place. It is a gift. It is love. The sinner is made righteous.

The second system is contrary to standard advice like the following: "If you want to be good at something, practice." A person is not born as a good woodworker. Rather, he works at it and becomes a good woodworker. A person becomes patient by practicing patience. This is a righteousness by law. While this is generally good advice for life in a sinful world, Jesus teaches the opposite when it comes to the Christian himself. On one occasion, he used an analogy of a tree. A bad tree cannot produce good fruit. Only a good tree produces good fruit (Matt. 7:17–18). The person is made righteous and then performs righteous acts. Justification (being declared righteous) proceeds sanctification (performing righteous deeds). Our towers of Babel, even the "righteous" ones, are attempts at self-justification, to make a name for ourselves, to be judged by our actions according to law. It's a dead end. It's the wrong system.

Martin Luther found himself in the wrong system in his early years as an Augustinian friar. He was a part of the medieval monastic system. When he entered the Augustinian Order, he pledged himself to God. His whole life was dedicated to the work of God: his time; his energy; really, his whole self. His ethical orientation was vertical toward God. Luther never did anything halfway, and this included being a monk. He took his vows seriously. He also took the church's teaching of *facere quod in se est* seriously. This doctrine can loosely be translated as "Do what it is in you."[4] Clearly, humans are sinful. Everybody knows this. So how is a human saved? Is it purely the action of God, or is there human effort involved? The medieval church practiced a semi-Pelagian doctrine. This basically means that God gives grace, and the human adds works to the equation. But what counts as a good human deed? Certainly, it cannot be perfect. "Do what is in you," was the answer, and God will not deny you grace.

The breakthrough for Luther was the rediscovery of the two kinds of righteousness. He was not righteous by following law. He tried that. He tried really hard, but what was *in him* was not good. He was a bad tree. He needed a righteousness "apart from the law" (Rom. 3:21). He needed something outside himself. He needed Christ. Then things changed for the friar. He was free from the debilitating worry of "Did I do enough to please God?" God had become a monster to him, a divine being dangling heaven above Luther, who could never jump high enough to grab it. There was always doubt about the motives of good deeds. And the very fact that Luther would wonder about his motives proved that they were not pure. But now, God was Father. Now God was Giver. Now God was Savior. Now God was gracious.

So what was the point of his time as an Augustinian friar if it was not to please God? To ask it differently, "What's a monk to do?" What is a monk—whose whole life, time, energy, and self were dedicated to God—now to do with all that time and energy? His answer was vocation. An ethical reorientation occurred. Good deeds were no longer in a vertical orientation (offered to God) but in a horizontal one (done in service to his neighbor). Luther was curved inward, looking for justification. When God curved him outward, he saw a righteousness outside himself. Now curved outward, Luther also saw his neighbor, perhaps for the very first time.

This is not exactly fair to the monastic system of Luther's day or today. Monks and nuns performed and continue to perform great acts of charity, add to the arts, make advancements in education, and produce handmade goods. Luther himself taught, studied, and served his order faithfully. He was not cloistered away, praying incessantly. Yet it was a real concern for a multitude of monastics (male and female) who left their way of life in the early years of the Reformation. What's a monk to do?

Luther's rediscovery of justification by grace alone changed his view of work (vocation). His primary criticism of the monastic system had to do with the doctrine of justification (humans are justified on account of Christ alone and not human action). Yet this profoundly affects Christian life. In his quote that starts this section, Luther states that the monks bound themselves where God had set them free (to man-made laws) and freed themselves where they were bound (acts of love to neighbors). Those newly released monks and nuns were free to carry out a myriad of vocations (mother, father, lawyer, farmer, baker, and candlestick maker). All this for the love of a neighbor.

We might picture God's love as a waterfall. It comes rushing down upon us. Think about what Christ has done for you already: he created this place, became man, lived a difficult life, suffered many injustices at the hands of men, was tortured and crucified, died a horrific death, was buried, rose, ascended to the right hand of the Father to rule all things for you, and is preparing a place for you in that heaven. It's quite remarkable. I don't know why we ever worry! Christ has too much invested in us not to finish the job (keep us in the true faith and take us to heaven). This is the waterfall of God's love that rushes upon us every time we receive his absolution, hear gospel preaching, and partake of his body and blood. Not to mention all the daily gifts he has given us.

I suppose we could try to return the favor, but it's like taking a bucket of water from this waterfall and throwing it up heavenward. It's not going to get there. Try this at home, and you will see the water will just fall back on top of you. Such is God's love. Think about this in terms of worship. Worship, at its core, is trust in God. The praise of worship is proclaiming what he has done for us in sincere thanksgiving. But who benefits from worship? God? It's not like there is a celestial bank account in which the church's offerings are deposited. Those offerings (an act of worship) are used for the benefit of the church and the world. Who benefits? We do. It's like throwing water upward. It comes right back down upon us.

God throws our worship and deeds back down upon us as gifts. Who benefits from prayer? We do. We are reminded of the great things God has done for us as we repeat these words and actions to him. We also learn trust, much like a mother puts words of trust and love into the mouths of her babies. "Say, 'I love you, Mama,'" she teaches her child, solidifying the relationship of trust and love. Who benefits from hymns and songs of praise? We do, and so do the people who hear these songs. Praise is also proclamation.

The same is true for all our work. Does God really need your work? Gustaf Wingren wrote a memorable line about this very question: "God doesn't need our good works, but our neighbor does."[5] God is not a narcissist collecting all the praises of his people and their good deeds to boost his ego. Nor do good parents look at the actions of their children as an avenue for their own prestige. Good parents want their children to flourish because they love their children. They also want their children to be good citizens and to love their neighbors. So it is with God.

We talk a lot about giving glory to God. It's a wonderful biblical concept, but it is shorthand. "We work for the glory of God" is shorthand for "We love the world without any thought of pleasing God, and this is to his glory." *Soli Deo gloria* is a Latin phrase that means "To God alone be the glory." At first glance, it seems that this means that humans should do everything so that God is honored. That's true, but don't miss the nuance. First, theologically we give glory to God because he gets the credit. We don't save ourselves; God saved us. Any doctrine that seems to give credit to humanity is put through this test: Who gets the credit (the glory)? If the answer is us, something is amiss. Second, not only is the glory of God in his divine majesty; it is in his love, specifically at the cross (John 12:23–26). A god who demands his people's praises and deeds only for the sake of his ego is not a glorious god but a tyrant. This is not the God of Christianity. God's glory shone the brightest when he died for humanity.[6] We work for his glory when we are so free from pleasing him that we get lost in loving our neighbors. Working for the glory of God is shorthand for loving your neighbor.

I think this is what Paul is after in chapter 12 of his letter to the Romans with this curious passage: "Therefore, I urge you, brothers and sisters, in view of God's mercy, to offer your bodies as a living sacrifice, holy and pleasing to God—this is your true and proper worship" (Rom. 12:1). First, there is an oxymoron in this passage, "living sacrifices." A sacrifice, by definition, is dead. We can use the word *sacrifice* in a broad sense, but for Jewish Christians living in Rome (and Gentiles too), the idea of sacrifice would have immediately brought death to mind. Paul highlights this by adding the adjective "living" to the deadly noun "sacrifices." When the Christian lives for someone else in vocation, he dies to himself. It truly is a sacrifice.

The other curious matter is the idea of worship. The Greek word used for worship in this passage is where we get our English word *liturgy*. The term has to do with service and can be rightly translated as "religious worship." What is curious is that Paul uses it to describe the whole of the Christian life and not just acts of worship. Remember that worship is, first of all, trust. Christians trust that God has saved them from their sins and made them new. The old person is a sinner and always will be. The new creation is righteous and cannot be anything but righteous. This sinner-saint is sent to do work in the world. When the Christian is brought to repentance, the old dies and the new rises. The selfish sinner also dies when the saint works acts of love, a fruit of repentance. This is to the glory of God. This is worship.

Perhaps then we should rethink the relationship between Sunday mornings and the rest of the week. I wonder if many of us think about Sunday as our time of worship and the rest of the week as work and play. Sunday is for paying homage to God (us to him), and Monday through Saturday is regular life (us for us). Perhaps it is better to think about it this way: Sunday is for receiving (God to us), Monday through Saturday is for worship (we to our neighbor). On Sunday (and other days of course), I am preached to, I am absolved, I am reminded of God's great acts in prayer and praise, and I am fed. I receive the waterfall of God's love. I throw it back up in praise, and it comes crashing right down upon me. The rest of the week (and Sundays too), I worship by carrying out my vocations. I am not so much concerned with throwing buckets of water heavenward but rather redirecting this waterfall of God's love to my neighbor. I can't throw the water up, but I can stick out my arm and hand and redirect this love to others. It will run through my fingers and pick up all the filth (sin) that is on me, but it is still God's love, as diluted as it might be.

A Reordering

In this faith all works become equal, and one work is like the other; all distinctions between works fall away, whether they be great, small, long, many, or

few. For the works are acceptable not for their own
sake but because of faith, which is always the same
and lives and works in each and every work without
distinction.

—Martin Luther

The term *vocation* has a long history in the church. Still today,
vocation often refers to the specific calling of the clergy class.
A priest's, nun's, or monk's "vocation" is a specific calling
into a consecrated life. It involves special vows and a change
in lifestyle. It is something *extra*ordinary. Luther shattered
this image of society by declaring that all distinctions fall
away when it comes to work. None is better than the other.
None is more consecrated (holy) than the other. They are
acceptable to God, not by their spiritual nature or because
of the holiness of the person, but because of faith. This also
means that all work is equally important. Both the priest's
work before the altar and the miner's digging are God's work
and therefore valuable. It is not an accident that the term
vocation, once reserved for the clergy, is used in the Lutheran
world (and beyond) to refer to all work.

Luther did this slyly with another phrase, "holy orders."
Taking orders is a reference to a person taking on clerical
duties. One might enter an "order" like the Augustinian
Order. There is a new order for life. We might even think of
them as "marching orders." A way of life is placed before the
Christian. He receives marching orders from God. Luther
added a section to his *Small Catechism* (a simple booklet
meant to teach the faith) called "The Table of Duties." In it,
he gave biblical advice to the Christian in a variety of situations (vocations), such as parent, employee, or employer.
Here is the subtitle to the Table of Duties: "The household
chart of some bible passages for all kinds of *holy orders* and
walks of life, through which they may be admonished, as
through lessons particularly pertinent to their *office* and

duty."[7] Notice the grandiose words like "duty" and "office." This is serious stuff. Notice also the jab Luther takes at the monastic system. Here are your "holy orders": father, mother, employee, employer. Forget about entering the monastery or abbey; these vocations are the true holy marching orders.

We cannot underestimate what this meant to the culture of sixteenth-century Europe. Three estates, or classes, were foundational to this society: nobility, clergy, and commoner. While a middle class was rapidly emerging, for the most part, a person was stuck in one of these three estates. Nobility was nobility and commoner was commoner. There was very little hope, either by marriage or by social mobility, to move from one class to another. The only way one could move was to take a vow of celibacy and enter the clergy class. Notice that this would mean leaving behind a God-ordained estate, marriage.

Luther saw society in three different estates. These estates were God-ordained and not based on pedigree. *Ordo ecclesiasticus, politicus, et oeconomicus* can be translated into English as the "church, civil, and household estates." These estates are for the order of society, and in each estate, God works through vocations to rule his economy of love. Each person plays a role in each of these estates. This is not an order of who someone is (commoner, clergy, or nobility) but an order of God's loving rule in society.

The first listed estate is the ecclesiastical. One might be called into the ministry (e.g., pastor), but a Christian is also a member of the church and usually a member of a local congregation. The second estate is the political or civic estate. One might be the emperor, a town mayor, or simply a citizen. No matter what, there is a role to play. The third estate is the household. I left the Latin above so that you could see that this household estate is related to our word *economy*. We tend to think about our jobs and our homes as two separate entities, but this would not have been the case for most in sixteenth-century Europe. Think of a family farm today or a mom-and-pop store of first- and second-generation immigrants. The lines between home and job are blurred. We think this is a bad thing as we consider life-work balance, but it is wise for us to think about the household as the fundamental building block for both society and the economy.

Today we might think of four categories as they relate to vocation: church, civic, family, and career. Every Christian is a member of the church-at-large and usually a member of a local congregation. In both, they have a calling. One might be a pastor, a board member, a teacher, or simply a member. Everybody (whether they like it or not) has to deal with the political realm. Are you a citizen, on the local council, the mayor, or simply a voter? Everybody, without exception, has a calling into a family: "God sets the lonely in families" (Ps. 68:6a). Most have a multitude of family vocations: spouse, sibling, aunt, uncle, cousin, and so on. The last category is a catchall. A person might technically not have a recognized career (e.g., a student or a retired person), but still, there is a vocation, a calling. For most of our lives, we have a job or occupation: lawyer, truck driver, teacher, or nurse. A student's vocation is in preparation for a career. She is working hard for neighbors she does not yet know. A retired person might volunteer or be called upon to help his former colleagues with advice. Nor should we forget about stay-at-home parents. A paycheck is not a prerequisite for a vocation.

It is not an exaggeration to state that Martin Luther helped reorder European society with his doctrines of three estates and vocation. The ditch digger was just as important as the priest. The family was just as important as the clergy. A person's value was not dependent on bloodlines or occupational status but on Christ's righteousness and God's use of the person in a vocation. It wasn't perfect, nor will it ever be this side of heaven, but this reordering had enormous ramifications for the economy, the state, the family, and human rights.

Nor is it an exaggeration to state that your life might be reordered (even if it seems to stay the same) by the same teachings. "Who am I?" is a fair question we all ask of ourselves. Perhaps it is better to ask, "Who has God made me to be, and to whom has God called me to serve?" You are valuable not because of your last name, your salary, or position but because of Christ: first in your baptismal identity as one redeemed by Christ crucified and second as a coworker with God in his economy of love.

Luther did not set out to reorder society, nor did he claim to come up with new teachings. This would have been a horrific thought to him. He would hate that we call them "Luther's doctrines." They are not; they are God's. So where does the Bible speak about vocation? Here and there and everywhere is the answer. Hopefully, you will notice the sprinkling of Bible passages in this little book and think about others as you read. I already mentioned St. Paul a few times, specifically his letter to the Ephesians, where we see the Christian's identity in both Christ (justification) and his purpose (sanctification): "For it is by grace you have been saved, through faith—and this is not from yourselves, it is the gift of God—not by works, so that no one can boast. For we are God's handiwork, created in Christ Jesus to do good works, which God prepared in advance for us to do" (Eph. 2:8–10). God both saves us and uses us.

Yet there are a couple of sections Christians know well but don't always connect with vocation. I am thinking of 1 Peter and 1 Timothy. In both letters, the apostles start with the theology of justification, whether it be in praise of God (1 Peter) or in contrast to false teachers (1 Timothy). Quickly the writers offer advice for sanctified (holy) living. In both cases, this advice is framed vocationally. Paul instructs Timothy about the ecclesiastical realm—overseers and deacons—and offers personal advice to the young pastor himself. He then speaks about widows and elders, which is pertinent to the church but also the greater society and the family. Peter's letter runs the whole gamut: royal priesthood (church category), kings and governors (civil category), slaves and masters (career category), and wives and husbands (family category). When we think of the Christian life, we shouldn't think of it as independent of others. There is always a neighbor. There is always a station. There is always a calling. For a Christian, there is always a vocation.

Neomonasticism

American Evangelicalism has spawned what may be referred to as "neomonasticism." Like its medieval counterpart, neomonasticism gives the impression that religious work is more God-pleasing than other tasks and duties associated with life in the world. According to this mindset, the believer who makes an evangelism call, serves on a congregational committee, or reads a lesson in the church service is performing more spiritually significant work than the Christian mother who tends to her children or the Christian who works with integrity in a factory. For the believer, all work is holy because he or she is holy and righteous through faith in Christ.

—John Pless, "Vocation: Fruit of the Liturgy"

George Will once said that American football was everything that was wrong with America: violence and incessant committee meetings (huddles). I wonder what he thinks about the church. It can be a very hectic, bustling place. But as Aidan Nichols quipped, "Unfortunately, the 'liveliest church in town' has little to do with the life the Gospel speaks of."[8] How can a preacher climb the pulpit and preach on the importance of being a good parent and then, after the service, announce a dozen events or meetings that those same parents need to attend? The implication is that there are two kinds of activities: churchly activities and everything else. One is of eternal importance, and the other is of little importance. While it is true that there is one thing needful (Luke 10:42), it does not mean that everyday life has no meaning. Think of the guilt a church bulletin can heap upon the faithful. Do this. Come to that. Donate to this. Volunteer for that. All this on top of being a worker, a family member, a citizen. Forget life-work balance. There is also a church-life balance, and the church needs you. Jesus needs you! It is a recipe for despair. Or just as bad, it is a recipe for self-indulgent piety. An opportunity to indulge and revel in your personal piety. An opportunity to feel good about yourself—*spiritually* good about yourself. You are the one who has it together, who can run a family and make the church successful. How lucky Jesus is to have you!

I say close and lock the church doors. No, keep them open for prayer and study, for gospel comfort and preaching, but kick the incessant volunteer out into the world. Don't get me wrong, the church needs volunteers, but we don't have to make work for her members so that they feel spiritual. Being a mom is spiritual. So is working at a deli and attending your granddaughter's flute recital. Those things matter a whole lot more than some committee meeting. The work will get done! It will. We'll call you when we need you—but only when we need you. Go into the world; that's where you belong.

There is something dreadful lurking behind the busyness of the church. We are tripping over ourselves to be more righteous than the next person. It appears that sometimes—and sometimes often—rather than being motivated to do a particular thing for the love of a neighbor, Christians take on

assignments at church to put guilt upon others in the congregation who do not share the same level of righteous fer-
vor. There is plenty of law preaching out in the world—it's
all there is out there, in fact. The church should be the place
of gospel, not more self-righteous law. The world lives in
the first system (a righteousness by law); the church lives
in the other system (a righteousness by faith). If the church
is the place to feel righteous (and more righteous than everybody else), then the church is no different from the world:
"Unfortunately, the 'liveliest church in town' has little to do
with the life the Gospel speaks of."[9]

Neomonasticism—that is, the idea that church work
is more important than regular work—implies that God cares
more about the spiritual than the physical. This is nothing new.
There has always been the urge for the religious to escape this
world, to cloister themselves away in order to be hyperspiritual. Away from the world, they can truly do God's work of
praying and praising. It can quickly become the place where
the hyperspiritual are seen as better than the material-driven
masses. It can also become damning if those "spiritual heroes"
find merit before God because of their sacrifice. But is it really
a sacrifice? It's a man-made sacrifice. A man-made good deed.
I would argue that being a parent or plugging away at a factory
job week in and week out is far more complicated and difficult.
I imagine that many overworked accountants have dreamed of
a quiet life of contemplation. Religious escapism is still escapism. Jesus said that Christians are not of this world, but he
also said that Christians are *in* the world (John 17:14–15). It's
where we belong.

Os Guinness distinguishes between the "Catholic distortion" and the "Protestant distortion"[10] when it comes
to a theology of work. The Catholic distortion elevates the
spiritual work of monks and priests high above the ordinary callings of Christians. The Protestant distortion simply
takes the spiritual out of the ordinary. And in a bit of irony,

the word *vocation*, which was once wrestled away from the monks, now refers to secular work only, as in "vocational school." Guinness, a Protestant himself, rightly sees the two distortions as the same error. The Protestant distortion "completely betrays the purpose of calling and, ironically, activates a counter-reaction that swings back to the Catholic distortions again."[11] Both devalue life's vocations for the work of the church, whether it be performed by the clergy for merit (medieval monks and priests) or by the ordinary to feel spiritual (laity in the church).

God cares about the physical as much as the spiritual. He is the creator of all. This means that there is nothing that he does not claim as his own. God cares about the small stuff. Of course he does. He told us so when he declared us more important than the sparrows and that he knows the number of hairs on our head (Matt. 10:29–31). God wants a clean restroom and a productive factory. He wants cars that run smoothly and thoughtful lesson plans in our classrooms. Of course he does. Our work matters. Novelist and playwright Dorothy Sayers connects work with true piety:

> It is not right for [the church] to acquiesce in the notion that a man's life is divided into the time he spends on his work and the time he spends in serving God. He must be able to serve God in his work, and the work itself must be accepted and respected as the medium of divine creation. . . . What use is all of that if in the very center of his life and occupation he is insulting God with bad carpentry? No crooked table legs or ill-fitting drawers ever, I dare swear, came out of the carpenter's shop at Nazareth. Nor, if they did, could anyone believe that they were made by the same hand that made Heaven and earth. No piety in the worker will compensate for work that is not true to itself; for any work that is untrue to its own technique is a living lie.[12]

Work matters. Quality work matters. It matters to God. Luther famously said that the angels smile when a father changes a dirty diaper.[13] God wants clean rear ends! Of course he does.

Why does God care about such small details? Because he loves, that's why. He wants children taught, and he uses principals, teachers, and parents to do it. Not to mention all the staff it takes to run a school. God wants people protected, and he uses firefighters, police officers, and a host of government officials to get the job done. God wants diseases controlled, and he uses doctors, nurses, and researchers to take on this monumental task. He cares deeply about the janitor's work, too, for the very same reason. God wants it all, and he wants it done well. He uses people to do it. He frees Christians from working for him so that they can work for their neighbors.

Chapter 2

Vocation as the Setting for God's Work

God at Work

> Here is real heroism, everyone agreed. Professional athletes and movie stars, accustomed to adulation, said with one voice that they are nothing—those cops, firefighters, and other workers at Ground Zero are the heroes. Interestingly when the heroes took a break long enough to be interviewed, they modestly put aside the praise. They said, "We are just doing our jobs." That is the doctrine of vocation. Ordinary men and women expressing their love and service to their neighbor, "just doing our jobs."
>
> —Gene Edward Veith, *God at Work*

The life of King David provides us with some insights into vocation: first, when he was chosen as the new king of Israel, and second, when he fell into temptation with Bathsheba. The prophet Samuel was the leader of Israel before Saul was crowned as its first king. We might say that he was the heart and soul of Israel. After anointing Saul, Samuel remained the spiritual leader of the nation. But later, he was called by God

to anoint a new king because Saul had turned away from
God. This was tricky business because Saul was still king of
Israel and would remain so for years. At the command
of God, Samuel traveled to Bethlehem under the pretense of
making a sacrifice so as not to alert King Saul. He made his
way to the household of Jesse. There he would find a new
king to replace Saul.

In 1 Samuel 16, we are told about this encounter
between Samuel and Jesse. Jesse's family would provide not
only the next king of Israel but eventually the Messiah. At
Jesse's estate, Samuel first saw Eliab, Jesse's tall and hand-
some son. "Surely the LORD's anointed stands here before
the LORD," Samuel thought. But Eliab was not the one. "Do
not consider his appearance or his height" (1 Sam. 16:6–7),
the Lord told his prophet. Even though Eliab had the look
of a leader, he was not chosen by God. Jesse had his next
son present himself before Samuel, but he was not the Lord's
anointed either. In total, Jesse had seven of his sons pass by
Samuel. None were anointed despite their qualifications.

Samuel then asked if there were any more sons. There
was—the youngest—but he was out tending the sheep.
Someone had to tend the sheep, and it wasn't like he would
be chosen to lead a great nation, right? Wrong: "The LORD
does not look at the things people look at. People look at
the outward appearance, but the LORD looks at the heart"
(1 Sam. 16:7). So young David was pressed into duty, eventually becoming the most famous king Israel ever had.

The implication for vocation is that God uses the ordinary
to accomplish the extraordinary. Sometimes he purposely
uses ordinary means so that credit goes to him. Think of
Gideon fighting with only three hundred men (Judg. 7–8).
God makes it seem so impossible that we have no reason
to put trust in ourselves. There was no way Gideon could
escape the conclusion that it was God who gave him victory
and not him or his men. He also uses the ordinary to be

close to us. We do not need to climb a high mountain to reach God; he comes to us in simple ways. We do not need to be in the presence of great men and women to see the face of God; he hides behind the masks of ordinary people. In this way, he is intimate with us. It also means that ordinary people are asked to do extraordinary things. Even if you do not become royalty like David, God still uses you for divine action. The rest of the world might not see the importance of your work, but God does not look at things the same way we do.

David might have been a man after the Lord's own heart (1 Sam. 13:14), but he was still a sinner, and a terrible one at that. His greatest fall came when he had an affair with a woman named Bathsheba. Maybe you have heard the warning about sin's snowball effect when considering the tale of David and Bathsheba. We are told the story in 2 Samuel 11. David was on the rooftop of his royal palace when he saw Bathsheba bathing on her roof in the sun (remember that there was no indoor plumbing). Like many powerful men, David saw something he wanted, and he took it. His lust turned into an affair. The affair turned into a pregnancy, which David tried to cover up. The cover-up involved calling home Bathsheba's husband, Uriah, the Hittite, from battle (he was in David's army, which was fighting in Rabbah). But Uriah was an honorable man and would not enjoy the comforts of home while his comrades were fighting, and the Lord's ark was residing in a tent at the battle for Rabbah. David coaxed Uriah to dine at the royal palace to get him drunk and loosen his integrity, but still, Uriah did not sleep in the comfort of his bed with his wife. The timing would be off, and everybody would know something was amiss when Bathsheba started showing her pregnancy. So David devised an even more devious plan. He ordered his army to attack Rabbah, the city they were besieging. All the men were to storm the walls but then fall back. Everybody was to know about the plan except Uriah. He was a sitting duck. He was killed. No, he was murdered, and David did it not with his own hands but with his orders.

The warning goes like this: it started with lust and snowballed into an affair, a cover-up, lies, and eventually murder. So beware of small sins; they might grow into bigger ones. But there is a little detail at the beginning of the story we pass over too quickly. It reads, "In the spring, at the time when kings go off to war, David sent Joab out with the king's men and the whole Israelite army. They destroyed the Ammonites and besieged Rabbah. But David remained in Jerusalem" (2 Sam. 11:1). Those last four words are haunting: "David remained in Jerusalem." He was supposed to be protecting his people. Springtime was when military maneuvering took place. It was after the spring grain harvest, and the men were free to fight. It had to be done. It was a part of their vocation as soldiers. If the army did not go out, their nation could be attacked. And it was a part of the vocation of the king to protect his people. But *David remained in Jerusalem.* He sinned against his vocation. He sent Joab to do his work. He neglected his calling. So what was the first sin in this snowballing of iniquity that ended up in murder? It wasn't lusting; it was sinning against vocation.

David messed up the order. He was supposed to do his job, but he didn't. Things were out of order, and disaster followed. This doesn't mean that every time we disorder God's order, our lives will unravel as drastically as they did for David, but there is a good chance things will not be right. Nor does it mean that when we keep order, our lives will be perfect. We still live in a sinful world. What happens when the mail is not delivered in a timely fashion? Businesses suffer, tax payments are missed, or the delight of receiving a letter, card, or invitation is delayed or never realized. What happens if the police do not perform their duties with veracity? Violence and crime spike. What happens if mortgage lenders do not do their job well and with integrity? Lives are ruined by financial woes, and recessions can devastate whole economies. It matters that we all do our jobs, doesn't it?

A Christological Endeavor

> God does not need our good works, but our neighbor does.
>
> —Gustaf Wingren, *Luther on Vocation*

Notice that sinning against vocation is always sinning against a person. Uriah was murdered. Bathsheba was enticed (maybe even forced) into a shameful situation. Their child died. Disgrace was brought upon the royal family. Yes, David sinned against God. He said as much in his confession to the prophet Nathan (2 Sam. 12:13), but it was other people who suffered. Vocation is for your neighbor, and sinning against vocation is sinning not only against God and his order but against your neighbor.

Before we go any further, we must stop and ponder God's grace in this sad story. After David confessed his sin (2 Sam. 12:13), he was forgiven. Immediately. There were ramifications for the sin. The child of the affair would die. But God forgave David. Just as we should not skip over that little detail about David not going to war, which led to his lust, the affair, and the murder of Uriah, so we shouldn't skim over this small detail: there was nothing between David's confession and Nathan's absolution (pronouncement of forgiveness). It is one of the most remarkable absences in the Bible. There was no "Do this, and then God will forgive you." There was no "Repent harder, and then God will have mercy on you." David was forgiven. He confessed and was forgiven. It was as simple as that: "Then David said to Nathan, 'I have sinned against the Lord.' Nathan replied, 'The Lord has taken away your sin.

You are not going to die" (2 Sam. 12:13). You and I will always be sinning, someway, somehow, against our vocations and therefore against God and his order and, just as sadly, against the people we are to serve. But there is forgiveness, and it is a forgiveness with no strings attached. If God can forgive David, there is no reason to believe that he will not forgive me, no matter what disaster of a situation I make for myself.

Now let's return to the original point: sinning against vocation is sinning against a person. Why does that matter? Sin is sin. It is between God and me, right? This is not the way God has set up this world. It's a neighbor-relationship kind of world in which we live. There is no such thing as a victimless crime. That might sound like hyperbole, but think about it. Everything I do affects who I am: what I eat, what I read, how much I exercise, what I think, and so on. And who I am is who I am to other people. Let's think about a crass example. Let's say a man watches pornography—a lot. Let's say that everybody in the scenes he watches is a consenting adult who has agreed to perform these actions by her own volition. A victimless crime, right? But you can't tell me that those images do not affect the way that man looks at women, including his own wife.

But why does that even matter? Why do we insist that people should be treated not as objects but as something more than animals? I have already mentioned that our value comes from being created in the image of God and the fact that we are the type of creations that God loved enough to justify. In vocation, there is an even deeper reason we owe respect to other people. They are Christ to us. When we serve others, we serve Christ as if those people were actually Christ. Jesus had something to say about this very matter. When describing the last day of judgment, he tells us what he will say to the righteous—that is, those who trust him:

Then the righteous will answer him, "Lord, when did we see you hungry and feed you, or thirsty and give you something to drink? When did we see you a stranger and invite you in, or needing clothes and clothe you? When did we see you sick or in prison and go to visit you?"

The King will reply, "Truly I tell you, whatever you did for one of the least of these brothers and sisters of mine, you did for me." (Matt. 25:37–40)

When you serve others, especially when you do not even think about it, you serve Christ. Vocation is a Christological endeavor.

Vocation is also a Christological endeavor because when others serve us, it is actually Christ serving us through vocation. Think about dining out at a restaurant. Your waiter is in fact Christ serving you through that waiter. Christ puts on the mask of the waiter. Conversely, the waiter is serving Christ, for he is giving a cold cup of water (literally) to you. Doesn't this change the way you act toward your waiter? Are you not wowed that this ordinary event is actually divine? Do you not cut the waiter a little more slack, making his shift a bit better, which in turn makes him a more delightful waiter to the next table? You may even tip better!

Doesn't this change his view of work? Does it not encourage him to take pride in his work? Is it not an honor to serve you, the mask of Christ? Does he not find more delight in his work, which in turn makes him a more useful employee, which in turn makes his employer appreciate him more? Wouldn't that be a great world in which to live? Of course, we don't live in a world like that, and the reason is sin—and not just sin in general but sin against vocation. Still, what a pleasure it is when these interactions occur. Christ to you and Christ to me. Vocation is a Christological endeavor.

Beneath all this is the fact that we are God's coworkers. This is quite remarkable when you think about it. I work with Christ and not for my own gain (that wouldn't be very Christlike). Besides, I already have heaven secure because of Christ—I don't need to worry about that at all. I work with Christ in the Father's economy of love. It is how he gets things done. God wanted you to eat out at a restaurant that night not only so that you could survive but so that you could enjoy his creation, and he used the waiter, the cook, and a host of others to do so. In your occupation, in your family, in your church, and in your community, God works with you. You are his coworker. That's how he gets things done.

This seems like there is then a lot of pressure on us as we carry out God's work. On the one hand, there really is. What we do matters a lot. It is divine because it is all God's work. On the other hand, a sense of peace overtakes us. God is working with us and through us. He is on our side. Teachers have the ultimate Teacher on their side. The preacher is a coworker with the ultimate Preacher who preached on hillsides and in the Nazareth synagogue. Fathers and mothers are parenting with the ultimate Father. Artists, carpenters, and engineers work alongside the great Designer and Creator. And always remember that there are countless people God is working through in their stations and vocations in life. I am not sure why we get worked up about matters at work, at home, and even in our society. It's not about us anyway. We make it too personal. This is God at work. He'll get it done. He will.

I mentioned the section of 1 Peter where the apostle ran through the stations in which Christians find themselves, such as in the family, in the workplace, in the civic realm, and in the church. It had a vocational feel to it. First Peter is also famous for its discussion on what we call the royal priesthood. A priest in the Old Testament was a mediator of sorts, the person between man and God. A sinful person came to the temple with a sacrifice, but it was the priest who would actually offer the sacrifice. The priest acted as a middleman between the people and God. In fact, only the priests could enter the temple. Even more exclusive was a special room in the temple called the Most Holy Place. This room housed the Ark of the Covenant. This is where the people of God entered the presence of God. Only the high priest was permitted to enter this special room to make a special sacrifice for the sins of the whole Israelite nation and this happened only once a year, on the Day of Atonement. All this was a picture of the ultimate sacrifice and the ultimate High Priest, Jesus. He is our mediator. He is the one that goes between God and us and makes things right between God and us. Notice that Jesus is God. So we have no barrier between God and us. We don't need a mediator anymore. God is our mediator.

This worship taught the ancient Israelites a few things. First, they were sinful (unclean), and they could not help but be that. Some of the rules of the Old Testament seem so odd to us. A woman was unclean if she had her period. A man was unclean after a nocturnal emission. Being in contact with death also made you unclean. These are things that cannot be avoided. We are unclean (sinful), and we cannot escape it. Also, notice the relationship between uncleanness and the cycle of life and death. Sin is given to us through our parents, and it ends in death. The second theological lesson was that uncleanness barred people from the presence of God. You can't go to heaven with sin; otherwise, it would not be heaven but rather this world all over again. There needs to be a cleansing. The third lesson was that the Israelites were unable to cleanse themselves. Neither can we. This has to come from an outside source. In the Old Testament, the priests did the work. Ultimately that was just a picture of Jesus doing the real work of cleansing all of us, including those who relied on those Levitical priests.

But there is more to the story. God called the whole nation of Israel a priesthood (Exod. 19:5–6). They were set apart. They were different. They were different and set apart for specific reasons. First they were to be the nation to bring forth the Savior of the world. God made a promise to the first sinners, Adam and Eve, that there would be a Savior born of their own bodies who would redeem them. God made this promise specific to Abraham in a threefold fashion. Abraham would have a large family and a land for that family in which to live. From that family and land would come the Savior. This is why, by the way, there are all those other interesting rules in the Old Testament about dietary restrictions and rules about keeping Israel separate from other nations. It wasn't that Israel was better or different for the sake of being different but that they needed to survive as a nation for many centuries to fulfill their destiny of bringing forth a Savior. You may wonder how laws against eating shellfish could accomplish this task, but ask yourself that question the next time you watch the parade of nations at the Olympics. Where is the contingent from Moab or Edom? Where are the Philistines or Babylonians? These cultures and nations are gone, swallowed up by different cultures and nations. But Israel still has a team. It worked. There needs to be a tie that binds a people together. Ancient Israel had its own culture that bound them together. They survived.

So Israel's first duty was to produce the Savior, but they were also to be a light to the Gentiles (the nations). They were to tell others of this promise. They were to preach. In this way, they took the message from God to other people. They were mediators. They were also the moral compass for the nations. They didn't always do well in this role (neither do we), but considering the heinousness of the ancient Near East, Israel was a beacon of human rights and the rule of law even if our modern minds look down upon their culture and way of life. They were a mediator. They were a special people. They were holy. They were priests. They were a royal priesthood to the world.

When we moderns look at 1 Peter, we tend to think of this royal priesthood language as individuals. We don't need a priest; we have Jesus. The temple curtain that separated the Holy Place from the Most Holy Place was torn in two when Jesus died on the cross (Matt. 27:51). The payment for sin was made. We have access to the Father through Christ. We are reconciled to God. We are intimate with God. This is not only true but foundational to the Christian identity. But perhaps we miss a second aspect of the royal priesthood. We are God's ambassadors in the world (2 Cor. 5:20), his mediators. How else are the nations going to know about God? They need preachers. They need Bibles printed. This is what the church does. We are also, as was Israel, to be a moral compass to the world. This is not the ultimate goal—forgiveness is—but still, we are to act as salt in the world (Matt. 5:13). This happens in vocation. It is through us that God does his work (not only of preaching the gospel but also of loving the world). We are priests.

Peter and Paul are on the same page here. Consider again Paul's letter to the Ephesians. The line of thought goes like this:

1. We are not deserving of grace, but we are saved by grace. There is nothing we do to earn God's love and forgiveness.
2. We are holy. We are set apart. We are a holy temple in which the Holy Spirit dwells.
3. God has prepared good works in advance for us to accomplish in vocations.

Read again St. Paul's words to the Ephesians: "For it is by grace you have been saved, through faith—and this is not from yourselves, it is the gift of God—not by works, so that no one can boast. For we are God's handiwork, created in Christ Jesus to do good works, which God prepared in advance for us to do" (Eph. 2:8–10).

God's Modus Operandi

> Vocation is earthly, just as shockingly earthly as the
> humanity of Christ, apparently so void of all divinity.
> In the crucifixion of Christ the divine nature was only
> hidden, not absent; it was present in the lowly form of
> love for robbers and soldiers. Similarly God conceals
> his work of love to men in cross-marked vocation
> which is really of benefit to neighbor.
>   —Gustaf Wingren, *Luther on Vocation*

During the last fall of my final year of seminary, a friend and
I joined a golf league. It was a cheap, fun way to spend a few
Friday afternoons. On one occasion, we were paired with
two middle-aged men. They were midlevel executives slum-
ming on this cheap golf course with two twentysomethings.
We talked throughout the round, and afterward, one gave
each of us his business card and said, "If you are looking
for a job, let me know." I remember thinking, *This is what
people in the real world must mean by "networking."* I had
never been in a situation like this. I was always going to be
a pastor, and so I went to "pastor school." I took the classes
I was told to take. Eventually, I would be assigned—really
"called"—to a congregation. I did not have to worry about
and never really thought about my career. Networking on a
golf course was not a part of my world and never will be.

Don't get me wrong. I was fully aware that I was not at
a private country club, and this was not the CEO of Apple,
offering me a six-figure job. However, I still felt a little proud
of myself for impressing this businessman enough that he
gave me his business card. Nobody had ever given me a
business card before unless he was trying to sell me something. Then I looked down at the card. The man worked for
Waste Management. His business was trash. And then it
dawned on me. Executives of all sorts—with their briefcases,

three-piece suits, BMWs, and expense accounts—still had to do something. This guy's *something* was trash. On the way home that afternoon, I thought of the titans of business, like John D. Rockefeller. I always pictured him and his brother, William, as sophisticated men doing sophisticated things. They were. But in the end, they still had to do *something*. They traded in oil and then made their way into banking. The grandiose lives I imagined them living came down to drilling and counting, buying and selling. Certainly, they dealt with complicated political situations and difficult problems that I could not solve. I am sure it was a hard business, but so is carpentry. The point is that the highest-level executive of Waste Management and the trash collector have the same business: trash. As extraordinary as we may see ourselves or others, we are still ordinary people doing ordinary things, like dealing with trash.

Our God is gritty. He gets down in the mud and the blood and the beer. He does not "slum" like the gods of the ancient Greeks who played with creation because they could not help but get involved in the drama, passions, and cravings of physical beings. Nor is he the god of the deists who created this place, spun the earth in its orbit, and then left, never again to deal with such a messy place. No, God is intimately involved in his creation because of love.

Since we cannot go to God, he must come to us. So God, who is spirit, must deal with creation, which is physical. God, who is *extra*ordinary, must deal with the ordinary. A modus operandi appears: God almost exclusively uses the ordinary to accomplish the *extra*ordinary. As sophisticated of a being as he is (and he is), he still deals with trash (and everything else in this messy world). So he became man in the incarnation. He lived a regular life of suffering. He died a horrific death. He makes sure that rain falls and the sun rises. He makes sure that spring comes after winter and harvest after seedtime. He is involved in the nitty-gritty of this world. He is a gritty God. In the mud and the blood and the beer.

We might think about it this way: if God is evangelical, then he is incarnational. And if he is incarnational, then he is historical, sacramental, and vocational. I use the word *evangelical* in its original sense; that is, God wants all men to be saved. He is about the gospel (*evangel* means "gospel"). Since we cannot go to God, he comes to us. This leads us to the next point: God is incarnational. He took on flesh. He came to save us because we could not save ourselves. This means that he is historical. He lived in a time and place. Christianity has a claim on reality because this stuff really happened in time and space.

It also makes sense that he would be sacramental. Permit me to use the word *sacramental* in a broad sense. Depending on the Christian tradition, a sacrament is thought of as a physical thing with a spiritual component. Lutherans often define it as a promise attached to a physical sign—a means by which God delivers grace when he attaches his Word to a physical element (think the word of promise combined with the water of baptism). Notice the physical nature of God's dealings with mankind. We might broaden the term to include the Word itself. The Word is physical or comes through physical means: pen and paper or airwaves beating upon eardrums. We do not search for enlightenment via a detached spirituality. God comes where he can be found in tangible ways. God is sacramental.

We should not be surprised then that God is vocational. There is a pattern of intimacy. He became one of us, "tempted in every way, just as we are—yet he did not sin" (Heb. 4:15). He continues to come to his creation in intimate ways. He speaks with human words. He washes with human hands. He feeds us with body and blood. The pattern is continued as he works through others in their various vocations. He is close by, even intimate. "Where is God?"

you might wonder in a dark moment. Everywhere. Lurking around every corner hiding behind the masks of your neighbors, the ones you serve, and the ones who serve you. The ordinary to do the *extra*ordinary. Hiding to be close. The spiritual attached to the physical. This is God's modus operandi, and it is an everyday reality.

Masks of God

> God hides in order not to be found where humans want to find God. But God hides in order to be found where God wills to be found. Such is the game that must be played with such seekers after God. . . . The reason that the Father must hide behind "masks" of creation, or the *larva Dei*, is that God refuses to abandon the world or its sinners.
>
> —Steven Paulson, "Luther on the Hidden God"

God is hidden throughout this evangelical mode of operation (if evangelical, then historical, incarnational, sacramental, and vocational). God hides behind masks. His masks include creation, the flesh of Christ, the Word and the sacraments, suffering, and vocation. God hides in each in order to be revealed. This hidden-but-revealed paradox is his part and parcel of his modus operandi.

God is hidden from us for a few reasons. First, we simply cannot know him fully because we are finite creatures. Think about a god who could be fully known by his creatures. That would be a pitifully simple and small god. We cannot even fully know the people closest to us. We cannot even fully know ourselves. St. Paul understood this when he wrote, "For now we see only a reflection as in a mirror; then we shall see face to face. Now I know in part; then I shall know fully, even as I am fully known" (1 Cor. 13:12). Does a child know everything about himself? Do not his parents have a better idea about reality than he? How much more is this true when it comes to the heavenly Father and us? We are also the children who think we know better than our parents. We just do not have the perspective, the experience, or the wisdom to understand. So God is hidden from us.

God also hides for our safety. A fully revealed God would blow us away. Moses found this out when he trekked up Mt. Sinai. He was not able to see the fullness of God. It would have been too much. So God placed him in the cleft of a rock, and Moses only saw his back. God said to Moses, "You cannot see my face, for no one may see me and live" (Exod. 33:20). I am glad that God is hidden because the alternative would be devastating.

But here is the paradox: God hides to be revealed. A fully revealed God is a naked God. A naked God would blind us. We would not be able to see at all. So God hides so that we might see. God hides so that he might be close to us, even intimate with us. The height of the paradox is that the place God is the most hidden is where he is the most revealed. That place is the cross. There could not have been a more disgusting and shameful scene in first-century Palestine than a crucifixion. We have sanitized this picture in art and jewelry. We even cover the naked God on the cross with a loincloth. There was a good chance he was stripped naked in shame. Crucifixion was intended to shame the person. In a very harsh culture, few would have sympathized with the victim. "He got what he deserved," they might say. The Roman Empire was quite adept at propaganda. Crucifixions were held in public places for all to see, as if to communicate, "Do not mess with us. This is what happens to those who buck the system." It is the last place you would expect to find God. It was a godless scene.

Yet the cross is where God is most revealed. Here we see how serious God is about sin. There must be a payment. There must be justice. There must be blood. The alternative is anarchy with little justice for victims. Here is where we also see how serious God is about grace. It would not be my blood or yours but God's. It's not the sinner punished but God himself in the sinner's place. We would have never come up with this on our own. Nobody would choose a dying God. It has to be by faith. The cross is also where we are closest to God. St. Paul states in Romans 6 that we are crucified with Christ. How could this be? It happens in baptism. We are so intimately connected with Christ in this act that we are crucified, we die, we are buried, and we are resurrected with Christ. Our sinful natures die at the crucifixion, and we are resurrected with Christ to live a new day every day as something different (saints). The cross is where God is the most hidden, the most revealed, and the most intimate.

Similarly, God is both hidden and revealed in creation. We need to be careful here. Certain masks can reveal certain things but not others. We navigate this by looking to God's Word, in which he has revealed himself most thoroughly and clearly. It's the only way we can decipher the cross, which we talked about above. Without his Word, the crucifixion remains a tragic mystery to us. We can gain some knowledge about God from nature (Rom. 1:20), but not everything. This is called natural theology. We can conclude that there is a divine-like being. We might be able to reason that this being is powerful because he, she, or it made this place. We might come to the conclusion that this being is intelligent for the same reason and is outside of time and space, creative, a person (or mind, so probably not an "it"), and a free agent—that is, nothing forces him or her to do anything. Since we all have consciences, we might also reason that the divine is moral, and so are we. If we understand that we are created in the image of God, we can see that we are also personal, rational, intelligent, creative, and made for freedom. Not exactly like God (especially when it comes to specific attributes like infinitude) but still made in his image. This has huge ramifications for ethics and specifically human rights.

However, something is missing from all this. It's love. We might surmise that this divine being we know from nature is beautiful (How can we not gasp in wonder at natural beauty?), but that beauty can be pretty wicked (hurricanes, tornadoes, earthquakes, etc.). We might also conclude that the divine is pretty angry and doesn't seem to differentiate between good people and bad people. The rain falls upon the wicked and the righteous (Matt. 5:45), and so does famine. In bitter moments, we might think that he even favors the wicked. In a dark way, I have thought that those ancients who practiced child sacrifice were actually pretty good theologians. Perhaps their line of thought went like this:

1. God is angry at us (famine).
2. We need to please him with a sacrifice.
3. He seems to still be angry with us (the famine continues).
4. We need to offer a better sacrifice.
5. What is more precious than blood?
6. What is more precious than *innocent* blood?

How close natural law can get us to the truth! How far from the truth can our deciphering of natural law take us!

So nature is a mask behind which God hides and paradoxically reveals himself—but only his law and only in a vague way. We cannot know him fully and will ultimately make incorrect conclusions without his Word guiding us. Good thing he hides behind other masks. This is where we come upon the hidden God revealed in the Word. God uses words. It didn't have to be that way, you know. We could have been left with the onerous task of seeking God through some sort of enlightenment. In this case, the burden would be on us to search within or outside of ourselves, in nature, for the key to life. Instead, God speaks. Again, we shouldn't skip over this obvious point either: words are physical. They are not physical like a tree or a person, but they are written on paper with ink. Spoken words create a sound that travels and beats upon eardrums. God hides in his Word to be revealed. The Bible is not God, nor does it tell us everything about God. The Bible can also be challenging to understand. Despite its clarity of doctrine, Holy Scripture is not simply a dry instruction sheet on how to build a piece of furniture. It includes poetry and apocalyptic literature. The reader has to dig and study, think, and pray over these texts. God is hiding there, but it is also where he reveals himself. God speaks. God speaks to us. This is how we know him.

God also hides in the incarnation. God does not ask permission to enter our time and space. He comes when he desires, often uninvited. Graciously, his entrance into our lives is for our benefit. He entered our world in quite a peculiar way in the first century. Caesar Augustus was at the height of his power, and yet he was manipulated to call a census so that Mary and Joseph would have to travel to the birthplace of King David (Luke 2:1–20). Herod the Great was just that, great. He had consolidated power in Palestine, even murdering his family members along the way—putting fear into all his subjects—and yet he was driven mad with jealousy over the thought of a possible rival, no matter how small. When Christ entered our time and space, things were stirred up (Matt. 2:3). Politics would never be the same, nor would the world's culture or way of thinking. God was on the move, from the temple to the womb of Mary, to the person Jesus Christ and the New Testament church. His footsteps shook the earth.

Despite all the grandiose details given to us through Luke and Matthew—the angelic choirs, the manipulation of Augustus, Herod's tirade, a royal caravan from the east— despite all the wonder that is the nativity of Christ, the focal point of the story is quite surprising: a little boy lying, not even in a crib or a warm bed, but in the hay of a feeding trough. What was God thinking? He is finally going to reveal himself to humanity in a fleshy way, and that way was a little boy!

Our God is a scandal. He is not one whom we human beings would rationally choose as the one to follow or the one to save us. Jesus made that abundantly clear when he described the cost of discipleship. To some would-be followers, he said, "If anyone comes to me and does not hate father and mother, wife and children, brothers and sisters—yes, even their own life—such a person cannot be my disciple" (Luke 14:26). "You will be hated by everyone because of me" (Matt. 10:22) was one of his final bits of advice to the Twelve as he sent them preaching. Those are not exactly the words of a rousing motivational speaker or a good recruiter. Yet that is who he is. He is a scandal to us.

It may seem a little harsh or even blasphemous to call Christ a scandal, but he said as much about himself through the inspired Scripture. In St. Paul's first letter to the congregation in Corinth, Christ is called a scandal: "We preach Christ crucified: a stumbling block to Jews and foolishness to Gentiles" (1 Cor. 1:23), says Paul. The word translated as "stumbling block" is the Greek word from which we get the English *scandal*. Paul was not using this term lightly either. Jesus Christ kept people from the faith. He quotes the prophet Isaiah in his letter to the Romans, referring to Christ as the one who would cause offense to those who turned away from God's grace to a religion of works.

> What then shall we say? That the Gentiles, who did not pursue righteousness, have obtained it, a righteousness that is by faith; but the people of Israel, who pursued the law as the way of righteousness, have not attained their goal. Why not? Because they pursued it not by faith but as if it were

by works. They stumbled over the stumbling stone. As it is written:

> "See, I lay in Zion a stone that causes people to stumble
> and a rock that makes them fall,
> and the one who believes in him will never be put to
> shame." (Rom. 9:30–33)

Jesus Christ is an obstacle to salvation to those who stubbornly hold on to their own abilities to earn salvation. If a person trusts in his own ability to get into heaven, then Christ is of no use. And if Christ says that he is the only way to heaven (as he did in John 14:6), then Christ is not only of no use but an offense to that person. Instead of the way to heaven, he becomes a seeming obstacle to it. So much so that he is hated and despised for his love and generosity.

Jesus Christ is a scandal, a stumbling block, and an offense to our human nature not just because following him might be hard and his mercy might hurt our pride but because his ways are backward to us. St. Paul uses the same scandalous word in Galatians 5:11: "Brothers and sisters, if I am still preaching circumcision, why am I still being persecuted? In that case the offense of the cross has been abolished." Paul preached a salvation not through works (i.e., following the law of circumcision) but through grace. If he preached the former, then the offense (scandal) is abolished, then it means nothing, and then Christ suffered for nothing. But this is not the case. It is precisely that offense that is our salvation. So there it is: the ugly, offensive, and scandalous cross as our ticket to glory, bliss, and wonder. He truly is backward to us.

In Christ, God is hidden. But Christ is God, and so he is also revealed to us in the flesh. He is one with us. He is the perfect High Priest who knows what it is like to go through what we go through (Heb. 4:14–16). He is close to us. He is intimate with us. When he is the most hidden (in flesh and specifically on the cross), he is the closest to us. And the only way we can comprehend this scandalous hiding-but-revealing is taking God at his Word. His Word (e.g., in Heb. 11:1) tells us, "Yes, this is true despite what you see. Trust the Word, not your sight."

Martin Luther understood this. Of all the things Luther accomplished, of all the things he wrote, of all the things that turned Europe, the world, and the church upside down, perhaps the most intriguing is his Heidelberg Disputation. He finally just said it as clearly as possible: "A theology of glory calls evil good and good evil. A theology of the cross calls the thing what it actually is. This is clear: He who does not know Christ does not know God hidden in suffering. Therefore he prefers works to suffering, glory to the cross, strength to weakness, wisdom to folly, and in general, good to evil. These are the people whom the apostle called 'enemies of the cross of Christ' (Phil 3:18), for they hate the cross and suffering and love works and the glory of works."[1] We simply have it backward. Who of us desires folly over wisdom and weakness over strength? This is exactly what the reformer calls an enemy of the cross. Christ is a foolish scandal to our state of mind. He is different from us. We are by nature theologians of glory and, as Luther concludes, think and do the opposite of what a theologian of the cross would do and say. We by nature say "Good," and God says "Evil." We say "Evil"; he says "Good."

It is only by faith that we can be theologians of the cross and call a spade a spade as Luther said above. Of course, being sinners and saints simultaneously, the addiction to glory can make even the strongest (or should we say the weakest) Christian do and say silly things. It is a knee-jerk reaction of Christians to explain away God's unreasonable attributes. We want to make him more palatable to possible converts, or more accurately, we want to make him more palatable to ourselves. What we change him into depends on our personal needs, the culture of our times, and most dangerously, the politics to which we adhere.

God, through his alien work of law and suffering, shows us that we have on the wrong glasses. We wear glory glasses. Through these glory glasses, we see the world through a law-oriented paradigm. Righteous deeds are good. Evil things are bad. But if those deeds are done within the righteousness-by-law system, they become pure evil because they work against faith. And those frustrations and tragedies that seem so evil might actually be good because God uses them for good. Think about it this way: if the goal is faith in Christ and the opposite of faith in Christ is faith in anything else (usually ourselves), then maybe God has to first beat the false piety out of us. God forces us to see the ineptitude of the law to save us and our incompetence to see clearly the things of God. He removes our rose-colored glasses of glory and replaces them with glasses of the cross. Through these new lenses, we see the truth: the evil cross is our eternal good, and our crosses are used for good, too, if nothing else, to drive us to his cross where he is the most revealed to us and the most intimate with us.

These three matters discussed above all come together in another mask God wears: vocation. First, the hidden-but-revealed intimacy. Second, the take-God-at-his-Word theology of the cross. And third, glory glasses versus cross glasses.

Have you ever stopped and thought about whom you are supposed to thank when you sit down for a meal? Is it not a little contradictory to give thanks to God but then also give thanks to the cook? Which is it? Is it God or the chef who made the meal? The doctrine of vocation says both. This is not a general thanksgiving for God's providence but quite literally a thanksgiving for this, a particular meal. He was involved in this particular casserole Grandma prepared. So we thank both God and Grandma. When you eat that particular meal, God's love is revealed to you even though it is hidden behind the mask of your grandmother. This is intimate. He fed you. He is just as present with you as your grandmother is at that table. This is a regular everyday example. Now think about when you have to visit the doctor or when your favorite teacher taught you. Think about the soldier putting his life on the line for you right now or the pastor who will shepherd your family to peace in the resurrection when you finally pass away. Hidden but revealed and intimate all at the same time.

This sounds nice, doesn't it? But reality seems to tell us a different story. Is the greedy hedge fund manager really the mask of God? Can we really say that the clerk at the gas station who is completely zoned out and does not care one bit about customer service is Christ to me? Yes. Those who carry out those vocations/stations hinder God's love, but still, Christ works through them. In this situation, God says, "Take me at my Word." He will keep his promises to take care of his creation. If he can be hidden/revealed/intimate with us at the crucifixion, he can be hidden/revealed/intimate with us despite our sins. So we ask the question again, "Where is God?" Here, there, and everywhere in a very special way. He is present in a hidden-behind-a-mask way. You are never alone. God is present in your life not in a vague way but in an intimate way, teaching you, feeding you, protecting you, building roads for you, cleaning your teeth, and even fixing the plumbing in your house too.

When we flip the script (our vocations to others versus God hiding behind others to serve us), it becomes even harder to fathom God's presence. God hides behind me? But all I do is shuffle papers around all day in my cubical. I am a lowly tradesman. I flip burgers for a living. Is this really Christ's work? Yes. Double yes. I know it may seem like an average job or even a below-average job. I know that it may seem like your work doesn't "make a difference" (whatever that means). The problem is that you have on the wrong glasses. Through glory glasses, we see what man sees. Through cross glasses, we see what God sees, or more accurately, we see what God reveals to us. He sees love being carried out. Even if your heart is not in it, his is. Even if you do not seem to "make a difference," he makes a difference. And you may not be able to see it. So hear it. Hear it from his words. Take him at his Word.

The last mask I mentioned under which God hides is suffering. I turn to that in the next chapter.

Chapter 3

Vocation as the Setting for Spiritual Warfare

An Ethical Reorientation

For you are doing no service for God if you marry, remain unmarried, whether you are in bondage or free, become this or that, eat this or that; on the other hand, you do not displease Him or sin if you put off or reject one or the other. Finally, you owe God nothing but to believe and confess; He releases you from all other things so that you can do as you please without endangering your conscience. This is so thoroughly true that He does not inquire on His own behalf whether you have let your wife go, have run away from your master, or have not kept your agreement, for what does He profit whether you do these things or don't do them? . . .

That is why no man can leave his wife, for his body is not his own but his wife's, and vice versa. Likewise the servant and his body do not belong to him himself but to his master. It would be of no importance to God if the husband were to leave his wife, for the

> body is not bound to God but made free by Him
> for all outward things and is only God's by virtue of
> inward faith. But among men these promises are to be
> kept. In sum: We owe nobody anything but to love. . . .
> In [other] things one cannot sin against God but only
> against one's neighbor.

> —Martin Luther

I met a navy veteran outside a hotel in California a handful of years ago. It was a lighthearted visit until he found out I was a pastor. He had been drinking—not just that evening but for thirty years. The hotel parking lot quickly became a confessional. His drinking was directly linked to his guilt, and his guilt came from his job. He had pushed the buttons that *killed*—not just soldiers but civilians—and he knew it. It had ruined him. We talked about what it meant to be a soldier. We were talking vocation, whether he knew it or not. But then the rubber hit the road. It was time to absolve. He was wrong to think that he was guilty of sin in this situation, but that didn't quite matter at the moment. So I absolved him: "I forgive you in the name of the Father and of the Son and of the Holy Spirit." I'd like to tell you that he changed his life, quit drinking, and became a famous advocate for mental health or something like that, but I can't. I don't know what happened to him. But I absolved him, and that is powerful—divinely powerful.

Sometimes we try to talk people out of their repentance and guilt. I've listened to many elderly fathers who felt like they failed their sons, who had grown up in age but not in maturity. "I failed, Pastor" is a phrase I have often heard. I've also heard from women: "I just can't keep up with it all. Am I a terrible mother?" and "I hate this person who abused me, and I cannot forgive. I know I should, but I can't." Our impulse is to console them with something like "You are being too hard on yourself. It's not your fault. You did the best you could."[1] And sometimes we should say those words—but only after this: "I forgive you." These are words of freedom.

All of the above situations are in the context of vocation. There is a duty to be performed and a neighbor to serve. When failure comes, we wonder where the guilt should lie. A proper understanding of vocation is helpful in this regard. Let's start with the quote from Martin Luther that begins this chapter.

As he often does, Luther says something outrageous. He implies that God doesn't care if a man leaves his wife. What? Doesn't God care about the family, about right and wrong? The point Luther is making is that a Christian is righteous before God no matter what sins he commits. What is it to God if a man marries or remains unmarried or even sins? The relationship between God and the Christian is good—period. This has absolutely nothing to do with the Christian's action and everything to do with God's action. There is nothing a Christian can do to halt the loving forgiveness of God—nothing. Christ is righteous in the place of the sinner. God no longer sees that sinner; he sees the righteousness of Christ instead. The only thing the Christian owes God is "to believe and confess." And even this is the Spirit working those good things in the Christian.

The alternative is a business relationship with God, not a Father-child relationship. It's a quid pro quo relationship: you do this for me, and I do this for you. We are obligated to follow God's laws, and God is then obligated to reward us; we work, and God pays the proper wages. What kind of father acts this way? What father holds his newborn child at arm's length and says, "Here are the rules. I hope you can follow them. Here are the chores you need to fulfill to carry your own weight. If you fulfill your duties, you can be a part of the family. Once your obligations are fulfilled, then you will get paid. I will feed you, protect you, and love you"?

How awful. The father is asking something of his child that the child cannot do.[2] That's not a Father-child relationship of love. It is a business agreement. How could we ever do enough? How could we ever know if God loves us? Is God only reluctantly blessing us because we have reluctantly followed his laws? There is always a lingering doubt, and that doubt is a prison.

But then Luther brings it back around. That same man who owes nothing to God—what is it to God if you are good or bad?—is bound to his wife. A man cannot leave his wife because he belongs to his wife; he is a slave to his wife. This is not the slavery we know, a heinous spectacle of human depravity made even worse by its devious justifications (e.g., this is the natural order) and often tainted with racism. This is a slavery of love, which is no slavery at all, but true freedom as sinners—now made saints—to fulfill their true destiny in Christ. The point here is that the man in this example is bound to his wife in love and not bound to God by law (in which there is no freedom—only compulsion).

Once again, Luther channels St. Paul: "A Christian is the most free lord of all, and subject to none; a Christian is the most dutiful servant of all, and subject to everyone."[3] An ethical reorientation occurs. The ethical orientation is no longer vertical; it is horizontal. The Christian life is no longer ordered so as to please God but is ordered so as to love his neighbor.

It is helpful to think about the individual human as standing before God (*coram Deo*) or before the world (*coram mundo*). When one stands before God, he stands without vocation, "grades[, or] differences."[4] He stands alone before God. God is not impressed by your last name, your occupation, or your piety. He judges you for who you are. This is bad news for the sinner. For the Christian, it is good news because she stands righteous before God on account of Christ. When a Christian stands *coram mundo*, vocation is at play: "The need of others is an absolute imperative in the life of a Christian concerning love, works, vocation, but it is counted as nothing before God."[5] Luther said it this way: "So the emperor, too, when compared with God, is not an emperor, but an individual person like all others; compared with his subjects, however, he is as many times emperor as he had people under him."[6] The ethical orientation changes from vertical to horizontal.

Gustaf Wingren makes the case that Luther believes that vocation *is* the ethical agent. Luther believed that it was always wrong, in every situation, for a man to kill. We may disagree as we contemplate hypothetical ethical dilemmas such as self-defense. We might even rationalize the taking of life in certain other situations. Luther flatly calls killing sinful. Then he states that when a person is called to a certain station/vocation that calls for the taking of life, the person is ethically obligated to kill. The Christian can carry out the killing with a free conscience because the station/vocation is the "ethical agent."[7] So the soldier must kill in a given situation. The jury must judge even though the command "Do not judge" (Luke 6:37) still stands.[8] Here is Luther: "This is why God honors the sword so highly that he says that he himself has instituted it [Rom. 13:1] and does not want men to say or think that they have invented it or instituted it. For the hand that wields this sword and kills with it is not man's hand, but God's, and it is not man, but God, who hangs, tortures, beheads, kills, and fights. All these are God's works and judgments."[9] This, of course, does not mean that humans are exempt from punishment. "I was just doing my job" is not an excuse for sin. On the contrary, humans are accountable for their actions in the context of their vocations. It would be a sin against one's vocation (and therefore against one's neighbor and really all of humanity) for a soldier to kill indiscriminately or for authorities to wage an unjust war. So both Luther's and Wingren's conceptions of "vocation as ethical agent" do not eliminate all ethical dilemmas. For example, we might disagree on the definition of what a "just war" is.

Luther and Wingren only want to say that Christians can fulfill a vocation guilt-free because first, the Christian is no longer in an ethical orientation toward God, and second, God set up these vocations in a messy world. So while it may be wrong to judge or kill, it is not wrong for a righteous God to do so. If God uses the person (in vocation) to carry out his righteous judgment, then the ethical responsibility is God's, not that of the person carrying out the vocation.

The ethical reorientation from vertical to horizontal does not mean that humans are free to sin. "By no means! We are those who have died to sin; how can we live in it any longer?" (Rom. 6:2). The Christian is sinner-saint and will always struggle, this side of heaven, between the old sinful nature and the new creation (Christ living in us). So there are still ethical issues to discuss. We have already seen that vocation always involves a neighbor. Therefore, sinning against vocation is always sinning against a neighbor. People get hurt. Notice that the powerful action of vocation (God's work through humans) can mean that a sin against vocation (e.g., abusing one's child) produces dreadful results. Vocation is powerful. Our potential for good is great, but so is our potential for evil.

However, the reorientation mentioned above does help us use the framework of vocation to navigate through the world. If I am free from trying to please God, then my energy is geared toward this life. And if my energy is used in a variety of vocations (for me, as a father, citizen, professor, etc.), then I am always neighbor-oriented. Vocation is where ethics is practically applied.

So how shall I see my neighbor? I'll use myself—a college professor—as an example. How shall I see my students? Let's say my goal in life is to advance my research, write books, and generally rise through the intellectual ranks in my field. But the field of theology does not lend itself to such an independent life of study. So I have to get a job. In this job, I teach freshmen. I get paid and have access to research tools (the college library) and time to study. But those freshmen! I have to teach them the same basic stuff year after year after year.[10] I have to teach them; otherwise, I am not afforded the means and opportunity to meet my goals. So how do I see my students—that is, my neighbors? I see them as a means to an end. I use them for my end. But even freshmen are people, not things. We use things, not people. When we use people, we treat them as subhuman. We *misuse* them. We might go so far as to say that we *abuse* them. Now think of how a boss looks at his employees or how a lawyer looks at her clients. Are they a means to an end? Are they things to be used? Or are they neighbors?

The CEO of a large company is certainly right to have her stockholders in mind when she makes decisions. These are her neighbors. But she must also consider the impact made upon her customers and those the company affects. These, too, are her neighbors. Her neighbors, all her neighbors, are the bottom line, not profit. This is a tricky business. How should a marketer, for example, operate? It is not wrong to sell a product, but manipulation does not serve neighbors; it uses them for gain.

Let's be honest. We all have seen our neighbors as objects. We do not need to be engaged in heinous exploitation to be guilty of using people. When we judge people, we are *using* them to make ourselves look better (self-justification). We *use* coworkers to get ahead. We *use* employers for personal financial gain. We *use* those under us to do our work. We *use* people. And when we *use* fellow human beings, we misuse them, and that means we have abused them. Even more heinous, although it seems outwardly pious, is when we perform good deeds for our neighbors with the motive of pleasing God. We use our neighbors for our own sancti-fication before God.

A proper understanding of vocation, especially the freedom we have in Christ's forgiveness, is helpful. It helps us see the neighbor as the ethical goal and our vocations as the avenues God uses for his divine purpose. We are even able to ease our consciences. In a lot of situations, we might say to ourselves, "I was just fulfilling my vocation. I did my job. I wasn't trying to hurt anybody." This might be true. But still, I know, there is guilt. That navy vet was "just doing his job," but it is a fallen world in which we work. So here we are, in a messy world, trying to figure out if what we did was right or wrong. Here we are. Maybe in the hotel parking lot. Failures. So how about this: I forgive you. I forgive you in the name of the Father and of the Son and of the Holy Spirit. Amen.

Virtue for the Sake of Virtue or Your Neighbor?

If you asked twenty good men today what they thought the highest of the virtues, nineteen of them would reply, Unselfishness. But if you had asked almost any of the great Christians of old, he would have replied, Love. You see what has happened? A negative term has been substituted for a positive, and this is of more than philological importance. The negative idea of Unselfishness carries with it the suggestion not pri-marily of securing good things for others, but of going without them ourselves, as if our abstinence and not their happiness was the important point. I do not think this is the Christian virtue of Love. The New Testament has lots to say about self-denial, but not about self-denial as an end in itself. We are told to deny ourselves and to take up our crosses in order that we may fol-low Christ; and nearly every description of what we

shall ultimately find if we do so contains an appeal to
desire.

—C. S. Lewis, *The Weight of Glory and
Other Addresses*

Do you have a maid? I once asked this question to a group
of people I knew. They would all reply, "No," even if they
did make use of a cleaning service. They were the type of
people who worked hard. They were self-sufficient. Asking
for a handout was not just a sign of weakness but a sign of
immorality. I asked them, "Why don't you hire a maid?"
Before they could answer, I offered a handful of responses
to the question. Option #1: Maybe it is a lack of money, but
then again, none of you are suffering in poverty. How many
cars do you have in the driveway? Option #2: Maybe it is
because you do not want to spoil your children. Are these
the same children with iPhones? Plus, it's not like the maid
has to clean their rooms. Option #3: Maybe you are a private
person and don't want a stranger in your house. Please, you
just posted fifteen pictures of yourself snuggling up with
your cat in your pajamas. You're an open book. Option #4:
Maybe you think that you could use that money for other,
more honorable things. Like what, vacationing in Florida?
Isn't your time more valuable than money?

Imagine a typical family. Both parents work. It's a busy
lifestyle. You are one of these parents. You come home on
a Thursday evening. The mail is stacked up, and so are the
emails. The laundry is piled three feet high, and Junior is
wearing his underwear inside out because nothing is clean.
You can barely see out the windows, they are so dirty: "When
was the last time we washed them, June? No, I think it was
two summers ago." But you don't have time to think about
that now because you have somewhere to be. You can't
remember where, but you know it is somewhere important.
Flute lessons? PTA meeting? Hockey practice? You'll have to

check the schedule and round up the kids, who are already exhausted but paradoxically pent up with energy from the school day. Off you go again, buying fast food on the way because a home-cooked meal is a luxury you simply cannot afford but twice a month.

Now wouldn't it be nice to come home to discover that some of those stresses were gone? Laundry folded, windows cleaned, dishes put away, carpets vacuumed, maybe even dinner prepared? Just once. Maybe once a week or even just once a month. Would that stress relief not help your marriage? Would that not make you a bit more patient with the children? Wouldn't your waistline benefit from one less greasy burger? Just once a month. It wouldn't cost that much. Would not one evening a month change your outlook on life just a little bit?

So why don't you hire a maid? "Because we clean up our own messes" is the answer. It's a pride thing. More than that, it is a "curved-inward" thing—a self-justifying thing. We work hard in this house. We don't need help. I do my own work. I am not some soft trust-fund kid. I am independent. I. I. I. We turn our work from a gift to us (we have purpose in life) and a gift from God to others (vocation to our neighbor) into an avenue of self-justification.

Now let's look at the situation through the lens of vocation. I am a father. I am stretched thin. We all are. If I am curved inward, I look at work around the house and say, "I'll do it myself" with more than a tinge of self-pity. But if I am curved outward, and I see the benefit my marriage and my family might gain from me being a little less stressed out and not so busy, I might just forget my pride for a minute and see an opportunity for love. It doesn't have to be about hiring a cleaning service, of course. It can be anything: paying for an oil change, hiring an accountant at tax time, mowing the lawn. Maybe I don't need to fix the plumbing myself. Everybody's financial situation is different, of course, and some things we cannot afford, but still, wouldn't it help not only your family but also the personal economy of whomever you hired? Nobody is purely self-sufficient anyway. We depend on scores of people carrying out their vocations. We do not and cannot do it all. You don't churn your own butter, do you? So why not hire a maid?

This is about virtue—or, to put it into theological terms, *sanctification* (the holy life Christians live as those made righteous by Christ). What is the purpose of your virtue or sanctification? What is the telos—goal, end, purpose? Is it virtue for the sake of virtue, sanctification for the sake of sanctification, or is it something else? In vocation, the telos is a neighbor, not God or our own virtue. My actions flow out of me with one target and only one target: my neighbor. It need not, nor can it, go beyond that target to God. Nor does the flow of love to my neighbor return to me so that I can say, "I am: I am patient, I am generous, I am loving, I am a good father, I am a good citizen, I am a good neighbor, I am self-sufficient, I am a hard worker. I am."[11] If my virtue is for the sake of my own virtue, then I have used my neighbor for my own gain. I have treated my neighbor not as a person (let alone as Christ) but as a thing—I have used him. Even if it is cast in virtuous terms like *self-sufficiency* and *hard work*, I use him.

The Christian is free from such a crushing burden. I don't make myself holy (sanctified) or even virtuous. God sanctified me. He made me holy, and holy people perform holy acts. Paul went so far as to declare that Christians are "slaves to righteousness" (Rom. 6:18). In this "slavery," we are free—free to love. But the Christian is at once sinner and saint. So there is a battle waging. It is a battle of death and resurrection. The old sinful nature is killed, and the new creation (Christ living in us) is raised to live a new life. Paul lays this out in Romans 6 in the context of baptism. Baptism is a death and a resurrection. It occurs once but also daily:

It occurs once with water, as an adoption into the family of God. It is done. It is a fact of history as real as yesterday's stock market prices. Yet every time there is repentance and forgiveness, there is another death and another resurrection. It is a daily baptism. Every day, I die and rise.

If you are baptized, think about your baptismal certificate. Mine hangs on my bedroom wall. I see it every day and am reminded of who I am. My identity is in Christ. Ultimately, I am not the sinner I was yesterday. To hell with that guy—he's dead. Drowned in the waters of baptism. Crucified and buried with Christ (Rom. 6:3–4). So every day is a new day, where I can shout, "Bring it on, world! You can take my wealth and my health. You can even take my life, but you cannot take away my baptism. It happened. It is a fact of history. You cannot unring this bell! I see the certificate right before my eyes." And then tomorrow, this sinner-saint will do it all over again, until one day, I will be resurrected into all eternity and the battle will be over.

Until then, it is a struggle, to say the least. Think about the sign of the cross at baptism as a twofold symbol. Many, if not most, baptized Christians throughout the history of the world had the sign of the cross made at their baptisms. It is not a necessary thing, of course, but a thoughtful one. Usually, these words are said: "Receive the sign of the cross on the head and on the heart as one redeemed by Christ crucified." Beautiful. I am tattooed with Christ. I have a new family name. I am branded. I belong to God. Bring it on, world! I am redeemed by Christ, and that happened at the cross. When I make the sign of the cross, I am reminded of Christ's saving action for me and my baptismal death and resurrection into him. Seriously, bring it on, world! But the cross has a dual meaning. It also reminds me of my cross. This life is not easy. Nobody said it would be, especially Jesus (John 15:18–25). I carry a burden. I carry a cross. I have been marked with it since baptism.

We call this "spiritual battle." We are constantly dying and rising. We keep sinning and are forgiven. This dying is first the hammer of God. He crushes me. He reminds me that I cannot do this on my own at all. I need him. This is God's alien work (through law and suffering) that is necessary before he can do his proper work (gospel comfort in forgiveness). But this dying is also for others. The cross has a new meaning in the context of vocation. When I die to myself, I, as a Christian, live for others. Here is the neighbor once again. I die for someone. The setting for spiritual battle is vocation.

When a mother sacrifices her time, her energy, her patience, her sanity, even her whole body for her children, she dies. It is a burden. It is a cross. It is a cross in the sense that she can wonder if it is all worth it. She might ask herself, "What about me and my time and my dreams and my goals?" She might wonder if she is still loved, still pretty, still valuable, still productive. She is burdened, and it looks, through her own glasses of glory, like death. But she must not trust her eyes or even (at times) her reason but rather put on the glasses of the cross. She must become a theologian of the cross and hear God call a spade a spade. God declares her death to be beautiful and her cross glorious. And they are. There is nothing more beautiful than a mother. She dies to herself and lives for her children. She is free from the ultimate burden because of the cross of Christ. Her cross reminds her of his cross[12] and, therefore, her freedom in Christ. She is free to bear a cross not as an instrument of despairing doubt but as a sign of love. She is liberated when she gives up her freedom for the love of her children.

When a soldier is injured, when a teacher stays after school with a student, when a nurse cleans up after a patient, when a construction worker works through the heat of the day, when a truck driver threads the needle that is urban traffic, when a carpenter takes time at his craft, when a salesman hustles for his family, they all die to themselves to live for others. These are burdens, but the burdens are light, for they all are working with Christ by their side, as coworkers in love. And it's a beautiful thing even if no one in this jaded world sees it that way.

The old man does not love the neighbor. The old man is annoyed by the neighbor. The neighbor gets in his way. Like the tyrannical judge in Jesus' Parable of the Persistent Widow, the old man puts up with his neighbor reluctantly. He only wants to rid himself of the annoyance. After the widow in the parable pestered the judge, he said to himself, "Even though I don't fear God or care what people think, yet because this widow keeps bothering me, I will see that she gets justice, so that she won't eventually come and attack me!" (Luke 18:4–5). The new man, on the other hand, finds the neighbor a delight. Vocation is the ring in which the old man and new man spar, where the old dies and the new rises.

The Devil's Attack

> We lapse into debilitating alternatives: fatalism (doing what is required by "the forces" and the "powers"); luck (which denies purposefulness in life and reduces our life to a bundle of accidents); karma (which ties performance to future rewards); nihilism (which denies that there is any good end to which the travail of history might lead); and the most common alternative today, self-actualization (in which we invent the meaning and purpose of our lives, making us magicians).
>
> —Paul R. Stevens, *The Other Six Days*

God is a God of order (1 Cor. 14:33). Disorder is a problem. Disorder is because of sin. More than that, it *is* sin. It's not the way things are supposed to be. God is a God of order not because he is a tyrant but because he is love. He wants what is best for us. The devil wants disorder. But he is smart—crafty even. He wants us to believe that disorder is order or that disorder is good. The devil wants to pull Christians out of their vocations one way or the other. But we have a gracious God, and he will use people in a disordered world to love anyway (Rom. 8:28).

Consider the example of a father and grandfather. Imagine a Venn diagram. The two circles each represent a vocation (father and grandfather). Both vocations (circles) describe the sphere of influence a particular vocation has toward a neighbor. In this case, the neighbor is a child, the daughter of the father and the granddaughter of the grandfather. Their two circles of influence overlap because both vocations serve the same purpose: loving the child. But each circle also has a space that does not overlap because the vocations are different. The father is a father, not a grandfather. The grandfather is a grandfather and not a father. So both might buy the child a birthday present, but only the father tucks the child into bed each night.

The first point to make is that the grandfather is not meant to be the father to the child. He is not her disciplinarian (normally). He should not make fatherly decisions about her. That's the father's job. Nor should he want to. What a delight it is for the grandfather to enjoy his granddaughter without having to worry (too much) about discipline or spoiling her dinner. He gets to be a grandfather. And the little girl needs that. She needs both a father and a grandfather. But what if the grandfather disagrees with the father's parenting choices? In some cases, he might have to step in, but he needs to check himself. He is not the father. He is not called to be the father. He must go by faith. God called this other man to be the father, not him.

This sounds nice, but we live in a world of disorder. What if the father is abusive? An alcoholic? Absent? Dead?

In this case, love demands that the grandfather's sphere of influence increase. His circle gets bigger, and both the granddaughter and the grandfather suffer from this disorder. The elderly man has to give up his time of leisure and do the work of a younger man. The granddaughter loses the spoiling grandfather because now he has to play the role of the father, or if he doesn't, she loses a father figure and only has an indulgent papa to guide her. Yet in the midst of disorder, God's love still is present in a variety of vocations. People step up where others have failed. The devil thwarts, but God still wins. I cannot help but think of Jesus' words to John about his mother, Mary: "Here is your mother" (John 19:27). Jesus would no longer fill his role as son; John would take his place.

Let's take this to a global stage. No matter your opinion of capitalism, most people would agree with these two conclusions: (1) capitalism involves a lot of greed, and (2) capitalism has been a driving force in lifting many (though not all) people out of poverty. Or consider the issue of pharmaceutical experimentation on animals. Again, no matter where you stand on this issue, most people agree with these two conclusions: (1) cruelty to animals is heinous, and (2) a lot of lives have been saved by medicines tested on animals. It's never pure, is it? It's never wholly righteous, is it? Our motives are always mixed. This does not necessarily mean that we should exit the capitalist system because some are greedy (very greedy). Nor should I insist that my child not use a vaccine that would guard against disease simply because the pharmaceutical company's methods were distasteful (if not immoral) to me. God still uses people who sin against vocation to love the world. Who else is he going to use? We're all sinners. Look what he has to work with!

And how wonderful it is to find the brave in this world, the ones who do right by others despite so many obstacles. The honorable soldier. The upright official in a corrupt government.

The good teacher dealing with seemingly relentless bureaucracy and angry parents. The police officer trying to curb his own prejudices (we all have them) while trying to also stay vigilant. The lawyer fighting for both truth and her client. Thank God.[13]

Once again, vocation helps in these situations. Vocation is not an ethical theory that provides a pathway to unknot moral conundrums, but it is a touchstone. The first question you may ask is "Who is my neighbor?" As we mentioned above, this might be a myriad of people. It might also mean that we may cause one neighbor to suffer for the sake of another in a complicated world. I might have to leave work early to be father, and my coworkers might suffer (and vice versa). The second question is "What is my duty of love to this neighbor?" Notice that the question is not focused on the Christian following a law but on loving one's neighbor.

Sometimes all we can do is follow our consciences and say, "Lord, have mercy." We can only go by faith, knowing that God will get his work done despite all of us sinning against our vocations, using people as things, and working for our own self-justification. But that faith is in a God of promises. He gave us his Word, and we take him at his Word. Gustaf Wingren once again puts it beautifully: "The paradox rests with God: it is *he* who forcibly resists evil through the offices of judge and executioner, and commands all persons not to resist evil as individuals, even though they be judges and executioners. For that which the office does is not part of man's account, but of God's."[14] Wingren wrote the above quote to describe the false notion that Christians cannot be in vocations that judge and kill (Luther's examples of judge and executioner), as if there were two kinds of people: one who judges and kills and therefore cannot be Christian and another who escapes all vocational responsibility but remains Christian. I think the quote also applies when we flip the situation on its head: How can God get anything done through us when we are selfish sinners? Nothing is pure. Vocation is the answer because it is God who is working. The paradox rests with God.

So when the devil attacks and tries to get you out of order—that is, out of your vocation—resist. And when you fail, trust that God will still use you and his work will get done. How do we know? Because it is his work, that's why. God's use of sinners is messy. On a personal level, this is spiritual warfare. It is a daily dying and rising. It is bearing a cross. But it is a delight because we are free from the burden of both saving ourselves and loving the world. We are only privileged to have a part in doing the latter. He will get his work done despite us. He promised. On a global level, we can at once fight against injustice and trust that God will use even sinful people and actions for good—what else does he have to work with?

Crosses Are Not Chosen

> The old man is characterized by wrath, envy, greed, laziness, pride, unbelief, and such obvious sins, which manifestly constitute an encumbrance on vocation and one's neighbor. When the demand of vocation and of neighbor is laid upon the old man, he is made amenable. These sins are repressed and give place to a gentle and patient new man, who receives his life from God's hand.
>
> —Gustaf Wingren, *Luther on Vocation*

In his book *Road to Character*, journalist David Brooks details how the great medical missionary, Albert Schweitzer, vetted candidates for his work.

He did not hire idealists for that hospital, nor did he hire people who had a righteous sense of how much they were giving to the world. He certainly did not hire people who set out "to do something special." He only wanted people who would perform constant acts of service with a no-nonsense attitude, who would simply do what needed doing.[15]

Schweitzer was practical. He needed dishes cleaned and IVs inserted. There was no time to coddle self-justifying egos. He needed people who, without thinking about their virtue, saw a sink full of dishes and simply cleaned them. Schweitzer was not just practical but insightful: "Only a person who feels his presence to be a matter of course, not something out of the ordinary, and who has no thought of heroism but only of a duty undertaken with sober enthusiasm, is capable of being the sort of spiritual pioneer the world needs."[16]

Crosses are not chosen. If we chose our crosses, they would not be crosses; they would be avenues for our self-justification. There is a profound difference between the two types of volunteers about which Schweitzer speaks. One group is curved inward; the other is curved outward.

Whether he knew it or not, the people Schweitzer was after were the sheep of Matthew 25. The ones who are surprised when Jesus says, "Come, you who are blessed by my Father; take your inheritance, the kingdom prepared for you since the creation of the world. For I was hungry and you gave me something to eat, I was thirsty and you gave me something to drink, I was a stranger and you invited me in, I needed clothes and you clothed me, I was sick and you looked after me, I was in prison and you came to visit me" (Matt. 25:34b–36). Schweitzer wanted the righteous—that is, those who are righteous by faith, who are not looking for a reason to justify themselves but rather are curved outward toward their neighbors. But it is more than that; he was seeking candidates who naturally were this way—that is, they had a certain character. They were free enough to not care about their image. They were free enough to see the work set before them. They did not choose crosses but picked up those set before them.

A cross is laid before the Christian in each vocation. While the Christian is free in a certain way to choose one vocation over another (plumbing instead of carpentry), the same is not true regarding his cross. The Christian is brought into work with Christ. He is a coworker with Christ and will suffer as Christ did. Christ did not choose his cross, it was laid before him (Matt. 26:39). Choosing a cross for oneself is no cross at all. It is a negative theology of glory—that is, an attempt to suffer for the sake of glory. "Look at me. I served as a medical missionary." To borrow a phrase from St. Paul, the Christian does not "consider equality with God something to be used to his own advantage" (Phil. 2:6). This passage is talking about Christ being of the same essence as the Father, but you can understand the connection. When a Christian is yoked with Christ in vocation, he cannot fathom what this means. He is not turned inward to muse upon this mystery but simply does the work laid before him, knowing that if he suffers, he suffers with Christ (Phil. 3:10).

This is the true imitation of Christ. It is not a curved-inward imitation. The Christian should not be consumed with striving to be like Christ for the sake of her own virtue. This will only drive the Christian to despair (if she is honest) or to delusional pride. Wingren summarizes Luther's attack on imitation:

> He regards it as the result of deficient ethical earnestness. The motive of imitation is not to serve others and to lose oneself, but to be just as holy as somebody else one knows. In imitation, one's aim is steadily centered in oneself. The object sought is one's own achievement of personality, and one's own condition is not the foundation of one's action but the objective of it.
>
> But for him who gives himself to his vocation, the gospel is the fountain; action flows from the fact of having been

saved. The gospel says expressly that one's person is saved in an eternal kingdom after death, even if it is spent and cannot be "saved" in one's vocation because it is completely devoted to one's responsibilities and tasks. It is one's neighbor, not one's sanctification, which stands at the heart of the ethics of vocation. By that fact, all imitation is excluded.[17]

True imitation is not concerned with imitation at all. While it is true that we are to be Christlike, it is not for ourselves. This is dangerous territory, for once we start looking inward to see how we are doing, we wander away from a Christlike life.

Nor can we be like Christ. This is true for an obvious reason: we are not God. But it is also true because we are never in the same situation as Christ or any saint who has gone before us. We are in similar situations, but each is always different because the neighbor is different. If vocational ethics is geared toward the neighbor, then we are always in a unique situation. Who are we to imitate? And yet we are always with Christ, our coworker. In this way, we are in a better situation than we would be if we were to imitate him: we are working *with* him. Wingren put it this way: "In a way, the law represents unchanging imitation, without regard for 'the time,' but the command calls a man to his vocation, which is guided by the need of 'the time.' In imitation the individual person is just one more number, but in vocation . . . he is a living instrument in the hand of a Creator."[18] A law-oriented life sees imitation as the ultimate goal, but a gospel-oriented life sees each neighbor as a unique person whom God loves and therefore each vocational action as a unique and intimate act of God's love. It is the difference between virtue for the sake of virtue and virtue for the sake of a neighbor. The Christian life is so much better than an imitation of Christ; it is doing Christ's work. We *are* the hand of God, not a cheap imitation.

We have a problem, though. We are naturally curved inward. We are always wondering how we are doing and how we stack up to the competition (notice that we make neighbors our rivals instead of the telos of our love). So God comes with his law and suffering. He reminds us all too painfully that what is in us is rotten. He kills us. He kills us to make us alive in him. Like Albert Schweitzer, he doesn't have time for such silly navel-gazing. There is work to be done. So he kills us daily and raises us daily. This is a spiritual battle, and the setting for this battle is vocation. So God hides behind that fourth mask we mentioned in the previous chapter, suffering. This is not pessimism; it is true optimism. Having already been crucified and resurrected with Christ, I have nothing to fear. I need not pretend like all is well or that the cross before me will be easy to carry. I simply go with Christ. What could be worse than the crucifixion I have already endured with him (Rom. 6:3)? I need not run away from the darkness. Instead, I am given permission to enter the darkness with Christ.[19]

Just like talk about "living for the glory of God," talk about spiritual growth is almost ubiquitous in the Christian church but lacks nuance. How do spiritual growth and maturity, both beautiful biblical themes, jive with a proper understanding of the imitation of Christ? It is helpful to point out that growth is always something we see retrospectively. Think about a doorpost on which a parent tracks the height of a child. A six-year-old boy is very concerned with how tall he has grown. He is impatient with his growth. He might close his eyes and say, "Grow!," but it will not work. He only looks back and realizes he has grown. It is the same with spiritual growth. We look back upon our growth and realize that God put us in the right situations and often curbed our enthusiasm. Only years later do we realize that we grew. And here is the thing about the doorpost: children stop caring about how tall they have become at a certain age. They have other things to occupy their thoughts. They grow *up* enough to grow *out* of caring how tall they are. Similarly, we spiritually grow *up* enough to grow *out* of caring about how we are doing. We are secure in Christ. We see dishes that need cleaning and just clean them without worrying about spiritual growth. Until the sinner rears his ugly head. So God kills us again and resurrects us too. And around and around we go until we get to heaven. Will we grow through all this? Sure, but not in a straight line. And who cares anyway? There are dishes to be washed. And children to love, leaves to rake, expense reports to authorize, fires to put out, and a world to enjoy. This is true no matter where the mark on the spiritual doorpost is. We lose ourselves. We lose ourselves in this beautiful world, and we lose ourselves in vocation.

Chapter 4

Vocation as the Setting for Human Flourishing

The Pursuit of Flourishing

These days our English word, "happiness," is typically used to refer to a feeling or subjective state of pleasure, satisfaction, contentment, or enjoyment—a largely subjective, superficial, and luck-dependent matter. . . . For [ancient and medieval thinkers] *eudaimonia* was seldom if ever conceived of as a kind of subjective state or feeling. It was identified with the *summum bonum*, the supreme or highest good, the objectively good life for humans. According to Aristotle, whose eudaimonistic views are probably the most influential of all, "*eudaimonia*" is synonymous with "doing well" or "living well" i.e. living the best or most excellent kind of life . . . Aristotle himself concludes that true *eudaimonia* consists in one's living a virtuous life—hardly our superficial and selfish notion of "happiness."

—David Horner, "The Pursuit of Happiness"

Happiness is another concept, like "the glory of God," that we hear about a lot but struggle to define. What does happiness mean? Like "spiritual growth," another concept on our lips and minds, happiness is one of those things that we look back upon. We tend not to say, "I am happy" but rather "I was happy." I am old enough to look back on the days when my children were young as "the good old days." Life was simpler then. If I only could go back. But they were not simple. I am not yet old enough to forget what I thought back then: "It will get easier. Once the kids are out of diapers. Once we have a little more income." Back then, I looked forward to happiness. Rarely do we stop and say "Right now, at this moment, I am happy. I have made it. Everything is great."[1] We look back with nostalgia or look forward in hope.

Perhaps part of the problem is our definition of happiness. We tend to explain happiness in terms of a personal euphoria—that is, how we feel. In America, we speak about it, or at least the pursuit of it, as a right. "Life, liberty, and the pursuit of happiness" is written both in America's founding documents and on our minds. But what is happiness?

Justice Anthony Kennedy offers a corrective to this curved-inward view of happiness. "In this era, happiness carries with it the connotation of self-pleasure; there is a hedonistic component to the definition now. However, that's not what Jefferson meant, and it's not what the Framers meant. If you read Washington, he uses the term *happiness* all the time. As did the other members of the generation at the time of the founding. For them, happiness meant that feeling of self-worth and dignity you acquire by contributing to your community and to its civic life."[2]

The founding fathers were familiar with the Greek concept of *eudaimonia*, a word that is most often translated into English as "happiness." It was the summum bonum—that is, the highest good. It was the telos, or goal, of life. All human activity is driven to this end.[3] For the founding fathers of

America, it was to participate in society, homestead, build schools and churches, start a business, and participate in local government. It was certainly not the right to pursue a feeling, one that seems forever elusive to the present, always in the past or the future.

Finally, eudaimonia, at least for Aristotle, was to be godlike and therefore beloved by the gods. This meant living a life of thoughtful virtue. A happy man thinks about the virtues and cultivates them in his own life. He does not get too high or too low. He does not succumb to the temptations of the extreme. He is thoughtful and kind. He pursues excellence and success. He is happy. Perhaps a better way to translate eudaimonia, rather than "happiness," is "flourishing." Eudaimonia is a full and well-rounded life. It is to flourish as a human being.

I wonder if eudaimonia is the Greek attempt at what the Hebrews called "shalom." These two words, really concepts, are not identical but have some similarities. Like eudaimonia and happiness, shalom has a one-word translation in English that doesn't quite capture the entirety of the concept. It is often translated as "peace." But it is more than the cessation of armed conflict. Nor did the Hebrews use *shalom* to mean a personal inner peace. Think of peacetime as opposed to wartime. Wartime is when the economy is ruined. It is when we are scared to send our children to school (if there even is one) for fear of sniper fire. It is when we wait for three hours to buy a loaf of bread one hundred times what it cost before the war started. It is not what it is supposed to be. It is the direct result of sin. Peacetime, on the other hand, is when schools are opened, the economy is rolling, the rule of law is in effect, museums are built, hospitals are funded, and the arts are appreciated. In short, it is the way things are supposed to be. It is the opposite of sin. It is human flourishing.

Shalom can be translated as "peace" but also as "security" or "prosperity." At its base, it means "wholeness."

Cornelius Plantinga offers this definition: "In the Bible, shalom means universal flourishing, wholeness, and delight—a
rich state of affairs in which natural needs are satisfied
and natural gifts fruitfully employed, a state of affairs that
inspires joyful wonder as its Creator and Savior opens doors
and welcomes the creatures in whom he delights. Shalom, in
other words, is the way things ought to be."[4]

Shalom, or human flourishing and wholeness, cannot
be reached in its fullness here on earth. However, this does
not mean that we shouldn't strive for and even fight for shalom. We should.

Jeremiah wrote to the exiles in Babylon, encourag-
ing them to seek the shalom of the city to which they were
exiled (Jer. 29:7). He first describes their own shalom and
then connects it to the shalom of Babylon. He encourages the
exiles to do the following: "Build houses and settle down; plant
gardens and eat what they produce. Marry and have sons and
daughters; find wives for your sons and give your daughters in
marriage, so that they too may have sons and daughters.
Increase in number there; do not decrease. Also, seek the
peace and prosperity of the city to which I have carried you
into exile. Pray to the LORD for it, because if it prospers,
you too will prosper" (Jer. 29:5–7). God encouraged them to
flourish as a people, reminiscent of his initial Genesis call
to fill the earth and subdue it. This was their shalom. The
prophet Jeremiah connected the shalom of the exiles with
the shalom of their oppressors. Here (in verse 7), *Shalom*
is translated as "peace and prosperity." In short, God wants
his people to do well. Shalom is what God wants, and it is
what God wants his people to pursue (Ps. 34:14). It is also
the promise of eternal peace God gives to his believers, ush-
ered in by the "Prince of Peace" (Isa. 9:6).

Four concepts are included in human flourishing: prosperity, security, freedom, and purpose. It is hard to flourish
as a human being if you do not know from where your next

meal will come (prosperity), or if you worry about being killed (security), or if you are imprisoned (freedom). It is also extremely difficult to even get out of bed in the morning to live a life of flourishing without a reason (purpose). The tragic nature of a sinful world is evident by the lack of flourishing.

The setting for human flourishing is vocation. This is how we have economic prosperity. This is how we are afforded security. This is how freedom is protected. And perhaps most importantly, it is where we find purpose. So the pursuit of happiness is the pursuit of vocation. Besides the forgiveness of sins (which leads to eternal shalom/happiness/flourishing), there is no higher good (summum bonum). This is evident to all. Aristotle labeled people who equate good/happiness with pleasure as "the most vulgar."[5] The virtuous good life seeks the flourishing of others as well as self. We are the type of creature, made in the image of God, who desires epicness, virtue, and finally, flourishing for ourselves and for others.

What our Greek and American intellectual ancestors miss is sin and grace. It was not their job to catch them, necessarily. They worked in the secular realm, so their job was not to forgive sins but to craft a virtuous society. This virtuous society always remains elusive this side of heaven. True flourishing requires freedom from the burdens of sin and death. It requires security in Christ and trust in God's prospering hands, even when all looks bleak. True flourishing requires a purpose beyond survival or attaining human ranks. The setting for true human flourishing is vocation, which is based on true freedom in Christ alone.

Purpose and Self-Esteem

> God chooses to need you so that you are not a waste
> of space.
>
> —Daniel Deutschlander, "The Gospel
> according to St. Mark"

Bryan Dik and Ryan Duffy explored the concept of calling within the contemporary workplace in their book *Make Your Job a Calling*. They divide the concept of callings into neoclassical callings and modern callings: "Neoclassical callings originate from an external source and emphasize a social duty. . . . In contrast, modern callings arise from within and emphasize individual happiness."[6] For Dik and Duffy neoclassical callings are typically religious, while modern callings are more secular and revolve "around the notion of self-actualization,"[7] a curved-inward mind-set. Despite their attempt to cleanly distinguish between two kinds of callings, they admit that research into the current workplace environment "paints a remarkably consistent picture" in which "a sense of calling is surprisingly prevalent."[8] People tend to view their jobs as callings and this results in an overall benefit to the worker and an increase in their productivity.[9] There is something about us that desires and perhaps even feels called to a higher purpose.

Dik and Duffy recall a simple but remarkable true story of work that fits into God's modus operandi of using the ordinary to accomplish the extraordinary. They set the scene of a mountain highway, a two-lane road overcrowded with late afternoon traffic. The traffic jam is made worse because of construction. There is the requisite flagman letting one lane of traffic through at a time. A driver rolls up to the flagman hoping to get through but, of course, he gets stopped. Now he has to wait ("You couldn't let one more care through?" he might ask). The driver decides to strike up a conversation with the flagman who just cost him twenty minutes. He asks the presumably bored worker, "I'm sorry, but that has got to be the most boring job I can imagine. How can you stand it?" Not only boring but dirty, hot (or cold), and also demoralizing. Think about it. The flagman is the only one there besides the driver in the car right in front of him, who is probably mad at him for not letting one more car through. But the flagman's response is beautiful: "I love this job! Love it. You know why? Because it matters. I keep people safe. I care about these guys behind me, and I keep them safe. I also keep you safe, and everybody else in all those cars behind you. I get to make a real, tangible difference every day." After a drawn-out pause, as if the flagger is trying to decide whether to say this, he adds, "I'm grateful that I was led here."[10]

Wow. All this man does is turn an octagonal sign from "Stop" to "Slow," but what is on his mind is his neighbor. You can almost hear him saying with sober enthusiasm, "These are my guys back there, *my* guys. And they need me." He makes a difference and he knows it, even if nobody else sees his job that way. He has a calling.

"They need me." Those are powerful words. In the quote at the beginning of the chapter, Daniel Deutschlander takes it a step further: "God needs you." If God wants those drivers and that construction crew safe (and he does), and he uses the flagman did get the job done, then God needs the flagman. Better yet, he *chooses* to need the flagman. It's an oxymoron: How can someone *choose* to need something? God, of course, could send his angels to protect anybody he wants in any given situation, and he does that too. But he chooses to need us in our vocations to get his work done; he uses the ordinary to accomplish the extraordinary. It's his modus operandi.

Now consider what that does to our idea of work. It changed the whole outlook of that flagman. His job carries importance, life-and-death importance. Notice also that he was "led" to this position. There is more to his job than a paycheck. There is more to his occupation than his decision. His work is divine, whether he articulated it that way or not. He has a purpose. So do you.

I tell my students, "You think that you are busy, but you have no idea. Just wait. But don't worry; you will rise to the occasion when you get into the real world, maybe have a family, and take on all the challenges of this fast-paced life. God will make sure of that. Just remember that there is only one thing worse than being too busy, and that is not having a reason to get out of bed in the morning in the first place." We need a purpose.

Every generation complains about the subsequent generation. Usually, the accusations start with adjectives like *lazy* and *spoiled* and end with grandiose words like *entitled*. I once heard a man in his early twenties talking about the lazy generation below him. I wanted to respond, "You should hear what people in their fifties say about you!" The truth is, this is all an attempt at self-justification. People say, "We had it so much harder than these kids. We know what a hard day's work really looks like." Maybe, but I can guarantee, the previous generation said the same about you. Those who grew up without modern technology roll their eyes at their children and grandchildren who did. Those who plowed the fields with horses scoffed at those who had tractors. And so on and so on throughout the generations. Unless you are pushing rock for the pharaoh in Egypt, maybe you should just count your blessings!

Laziness is an easy and thoughtless accusation. It may be true, but there is most likely something else going on with your child who plays video games all day. It has to do with motivation—or better yet, purpose. Does your child have a telos, a goal, an end? We often equate laziness with sloth, but they are not the same. Sloth is, perhaps, a better descriptor for this. Sloth is one of the seven deadly sins according to the Roman Catholic Church: "Acedia or spiritual sloth goes so far to refuse the joy that comes from God and to be repelled by divine goodness."[11] We can bypass the theological discussion of this definition for now and simply note that we need a reason to get out of bed in the morning. We need purpose.

Considering our desire for epicness: as beings created in the image of God our purpose needs to be an important purpose. But we all can't be the president of the United States or a CEO of a Fortune 500 company. The question "Does what I do even matter?" is not far from the question "Do I matter?" One way to solve this existential problem is to pretend like our jobs have nothing to do with our value. But this means that the vast majority of our time and energy is wasted on something that doesn't matter except in that it provides a paycheck. That's not a satisfying answer. The vocational response is to repeat what God has already said, that every person and each job matters. No, not everybody gets to be a senator. Somebody has to staple and collate. And if nobody stapled and collated, or provided security, or cooked, or cleaned, the United States Senate could not function at all. It matters. Your work matters.

This is not an empty platitude to make yourself feel better. It's true. You may not feel that your work (or life) matters but that is not your judgment to make. It is God's. He says it matters. Period. Consider just a few things God accomplishes. He prevents disease. How? Through doctors and researchers? Yes. But also through janitors and garbage collectors. He brings great joy to his people through arts, leisure, sports, and entertainment. How? Through authors, artists, singers, and athletes? Yes. But also through ushers and ticket takers at stadiums and theaters. Not to mention those who take care of the lighting, the recording, and the sound. How about this one: God creates people, body and soul. How? Through mothers. Stop and ponder that. Mothers are coworkers with God in the creation of humans.[12] Gene Edward Veith described the lifting up of humanity in vocation this way,

> Luther's doctrine of "vocation" may be one of his most original contributions to understanding spiritual life. If he is critical of mystical ascents to the divine, insisting instead that God descends to the sinner in the means of grace, Luther goes on to lay the groundwork for what he called a mysticism of ordinary life. If he denies that salvation is a result of our good works, insisting that forgiveness is a free gift, Luther's doctrine of vocation gives good works a very different spiritual significance. If he sometimes minimizes human beings as radically sinful and limited, in his doctrine of vocation, he exalts human beings to a startling degree.[13]

"To a startling degree" indeed.

This purpose changes everything. It changes the way we look at our life's work, our day-to-day lives, and our self-esteem. It is quite a game changer to look at an occupation as a calling instead of a job or even a career. This is, admittedly, easy for me because I am a pastor. You do not enter the ministry (or at least, you shouldn't) thinking that it is a career. I even bristle at the terms *my ministry* or *your ministry*. I've never thought of it that way. It's Christ's ministry. I am not looking for a promotion. I've never had to worry about a career path. Where else would I go? On day one, I was already at the top of my profession. I was already baptizing babies, preaching, teaching, comforting the sick and dying, and offering the gospel to those who mourn. There was no promotion to be offered.

I fully understand that it is easier for a pastor to see his job as a divine calling than it is for a factory worker. And yet it doesn't have to be that much different. I am certainly not disparaging those who think about the advancement of their careers. It is an honorable thing to work for and be honored with a promotion or even a new job at a different company.[14] And certainly, there are other vocations to think about, such as parenting: a new job may mean a better life for a family. However, if your life's work (telos) is to make more money and have more prestige, you are missing out. The work becomes a means to that end. First, the end is no longer your neighbor. Even the wealthiest and most successful of all humans can wonder at the end of life, "What did I accomplish? Did it even matter?" Second, you may be robbing yourself of getting lost in your craft. If you are only working for the weekend (and retirement), your workweek (and life of work) becomes a burden devoid of joy and real purpose. Since your work life will most likely account for the majority of your time awake here on earth, most of your time will be joyless and even purposeless.

It has often been said that if you love what you do, you will not work a day in your life. But I love being a parent, and that doesn't mean it isn't work. There is something amiss with that common phrase. It implies that work is bad. Perhaps there is a better way to think about it: a good day is when you look at the clock at ten o'clock and think to yourself "It's already ten! I have so much to do" instead of "It's only ten! I could have sworn it was lunchtime already." It is the difference between feeling driven to accomplish a task (even if the job is a burden) and dreading every moment (even if the job is easy). Work can be good—so good that it drives us to labor regardless of the salary, prestige, or award. We might even stop watching the clock! Vocation centers our occupations on the work itself (and our neighbor) and not the drudgery of working for the weekend.

Our self-esteem, whether we like it or not, has a lot to do with our work. A snub at our jobs (or a promotion) can affect the perceptions we have of ourselves. As we mentioned before, the mere accolades of men will never satisfy humans created in the image of God. At the same time, we are the types of beings that seek to be justified, as we also mentioned before. We are lying to ourselves when we say, "I don't care what people say about me." Of course we do. Nobody wakes up in the morning and says, "I hope people devalue me today." I am afraid that the vast majority of us are always comparing ourselves to others. Where do I stack up? If we are honest, not always well. We remedy this by making our own judgments (others decrease so I might increase [John 3:30]). Or worse, if we are truly honest about our frailty and depravity, we can slip easily into despair. It is a no-win situation: we seek accolades that will never satisfy us.

There is a true remedy to our conundrum. It is a Christ solution. We are valued by God himself. What could man ever do for me that compares with the actions of Christ for me? Here lies my true self-esteem. It lies outside of me. My purpose through my vocation lifts me to a startling degree as well. This is the only way we can "not care what others think": by knowing what God thinks. With the righteousness of Christ covering my sinfulness, my destiny secure, and my profound purpose in vocation, I am free from superficially judging and worrying about my value. Here is where I find true self-esteem. Only the old man (the sinful nature) asks if he is righteous[15] in an attempt at self-justification; the new man (the saint) is secure and free.

Honor and Craft

> Faith, however, is a divine work in us which changes us and makes us to be born anew of God, John 1[:12–13]. It kills the old Adam and makes us altogether different men, in heart and spirit and mind and powers; and it brings with it the Holy Spirit. O it is a living, busy, active, mighty thing, this faith. It is impossible for it not to be doing good works incessantly. It does not

> ask whether good works are to be done, but before
> the question is asked, it has already done them, and is
> constantly doing them.
>
> —Martin Luther

It is hard to put into the words the honor it is to be a part of God's economy of love in vocation. The closest thing I think of is this: Imagine meeting a marine in his dress blues. You can't think of anything more profound to say than "Thank you for your service." If he is having a good day, the marine might respond, "It's not about me. It was a privilege to be a part of something bigger than myself." The "something bigger" is the cause of freedom around the world. What he means is that he plays a small part in something more profound than his individual self. And yet his identity is not lost in this "something bigger"; it's not as if he is only a number. Rather, he is elevated beyond himself to something greater. It is an honor.

This honor is true of every vocation. God wants my wife to be loved, adored, encouraged, taken care of, and respected. And he has chosen me for the task. There is a greater cause. The "cause" is the divine love of my wife. I am only privileged to be a part of the equation as God puts me on as his mask to love, adore, encourage, take care of, and respect my wife. It is a privilege. It is an honor. So is your job, no matter what it is. I don't deserve to be the husband of my wife. This is God's work. Who am I? The honorable marine would agree: "I didn't deserve this honor." The mother doesn't deserve to be a part of God's creation of souls. The musician doesn't deserve to be a part of God bringing joy to the world. The bus driver doesn't deserve to be a bus driver. All these vocations are higher than us. We are lifted up into them. They are divine. It's a privilege to be God's coworker. It's the highest honor. There is no stooping low into a job that is beneath us. All vocations are higher than us. We are all lifted to a startling degree.

We are warned in the Bible and elsewhere about pride. It comes before the fall (Prov. 16:18). But pride itself is not wrong. Pride, in a negative sense, is really the result of self-justification. When we are proud of our actions for the sake of our own virtue, then it is sinful. It is curved inward. The telos (goal) is self and not our neighbor. But when the goal is our neighbor, pride is good. It is good and right and beautiful to take pride in our work. All of our work.

Taking pride in work means giving thought to the craft of our work. This is much easier for occupations that require working with one's hands. It is easy for a construction worker to point I say, "I built that." It is hard for a middle manager to point and say, "I did that." Matthew Crawford, speaking from a secular point of view, recounts his own story of moving from a white-collar job to a blue-collar job. Crawford is a college graduate who worked for a Washington, DC, think tank until one day he quit to become a motorcycle mechanic.[16] This odyssey led him to believe the inversion of the common opinion that a white-collar job is superior to a blue-collar job. Crawford claims that the idea that white-collar work is cerebral work while blue-collar work is just physical work is false. Crawford, having worked in a variety of both white- and blue-collar settings, has found "manual work more engaging *intellectually*."[17] The modern mechanic is often engaged in as much problem solving as a specialized doctor. Crawford speaks against the unhealthy separation of thinking and doing (in both white-collar and blue-collar jobs) that leads to poor work and unfulfilled workers.[18]

Crawford also takes aim at another misconception, the idea that a liberal arts degree means an open future, while learning a skill or trade determines the worker's future. Again, the reality of the contemporary economy tells a different story. Crawford writes, "While a flood of college graduates look for jobs befitting their degrees, many of their high school classmates have been making very good money working with their hands for years."[19]

Finally, Crawford points out that white-collar managers have a difficult time determining success as compared to blue-collar foremen. The latter can go home at night with a good idea about whether he succeeded or failed. Either the motor works, or it doesn't. Either the building was built properly, or it was not. Not to mention that there is real, tangible evidence of the day's work. In contrast,

> American businesses have shifted their focus from the production of goods (now done elsewhere) to the projection of brands, that is, states of mind in the consumer, and this shift finds its correlate in the production of mentalities in workers. Process becomes more important than product and is to be optimized through management techniques that work on a deeper level than the curses of a foreman. Further, though the demands made on workers are invariably justified in terms of their contribution to the bottom line, in fact, such calculations are difficult to make; the chain of means-ends reasoning becomes opaque, and this opens the way for work to become a rather moralistic place.[20]

The moralism of the office, as Crawford calls it, has more to do with emotional intelligence than actual competencies. The manager is more of a life coach than a boss.[21]

Crawford believes that these flaws lead to a lack of personal responsibility, the manipulation of artificial self-esteem, and even bitterness toward work. He contrasts the idea of teamwork and a crew. If workers are only a team, then each person cannot stand alone. On a crew, while needing one another, each person stands alone. A mason is a mason by himself, and objective standards judge his work. Crawford connects this to free speech:

The difference is that on such a crew, you have grounds for knowing your own worth independent of others, and it is the same grounds on which others will make their judgments. Either you can bend conduits or you can't, and this is plain. So there is less reason to manage appearances. There is real freedom of speech on a jobsite, which reverberates outward and sustains a wider liberality.[22]

This wider liberality encourages creativity and personal responsibility as well. In contrast, artificial self-esteem, not based on objective standards, is easily manipulated.[23] Leadership can often turn into a Machiavellian exercise. A stifling atmosphere is easily created in which countless regulations, codes, and policies become necessary to manage the workforce.[24] Crawford sees negative results not only at the office but at the worker's leisure as well. The manager needs to work on his vacation (e.g., climb a mountain) because he needs to recharge while the craftsman is fulfilled in his work and is able to actually relax. The tradesman is not working so that he can live on the weekend; he is alive during both the workweek and the weekend. While the tradesman already knows who he is, the manager tries desperately to find reality, his true self, during his minimal time away from work.[25]

Crawford, without using the same language, desires human flourishing in the workplace. Work and soul go together—hence the title of his book, *Shop Class as Soulcraft*. Certainly, it would be better if everybody could see their work in a deeply satisfying way. Honor in work is easier to attain if there are tangible results and objective measurements. Yet Crawford misses the point that there is still a need for those whose work does not produce such tangible results, like the purring engine he himself fixed in his garage. These, too, are vocations with particular crosses. These vocations can be fulfilled with love as well. Loving one's neighbor is still the key ethic in such vocations.

I believe we can find pride and honor in any work. We can even think of the "craft" of any vocation. Let's say you are an accountant for a retail store. The CEO requests a snapshot of the monthly financials on one sheet of paper. He wants to take a quick look at the financial situation. "Everything on one page," he demands. Not easy. So you crunch the numbers and you adjust the columns and rows on the spreadsheet. When you are done, you take a look at the one-page summary and, with your accountant's mind, consider it a work of art, exactly what the boss needs. No needless information but everything the boss needs to make decisions. You get into his mind. You know how he thinks. You also use your expertise to show him what he needs to know. There is a craft, even an art, to this task. Now let's say the boss takes a three-minute look at your labor, says "OK," tosses the paper into the "to be shredded" bin, and moves on to his next agenda item. He did not see the spreadsheet as a work of love or as a fruit of labor, let alone as a piece of art. But you did. And so did God. You take the proper pride in your craft even if it does not get the recognition it deserved.

I once walked into a public bathroom in which two janitors were talking, one old, one young. The older man was training the newbie. He was waxing poetic about how to clean the bathroom: "Start here. Don't forget about this. This is how I do it." His voice was prideful. He was talking about his craft. It's true of your bathroom too. When it is time to clean your bathroom, you put on the rubber gloves and get to work. You have done this before, and you have a system. Start with the mirror and work your way down. Everything you do is meticulous. You even take the little plastic caps that cover the bolts on the bottom of the toilet to really get the bathroom clean. It is a labor of love. And there is a system to your work, even a craft. So what if the kids come home and destroy the place in five minutes? So what if they didn't understand how much pride you took or how important it was for their health and well-being? God knows, and so do you. God smiles at a clean bathroom, and so do you.

It is a good day when we get lost in our work. Those are the days that do not drag on but fly by quickly. Have you ever talked to a farmer about his work? Or a mechanic? A nurse? A stockbroker? If they take pride in their craft, they can talk for hours about the nuances of their occupations: the struggles, the technological advancements, the right way to do things and the wrong way. Everybody can "talk shop," even the janitor. Everybody can get lost in the craft of their job. That is when "time flies" in a good way.

Here is where true self-esteem in work starts. First, my job is important. God said so. Second, there is a right way to perform my tasks. Third, I can become an expert at my job. Fourth, I know that I am making a difference because it is God's work. Finally, I can take pride in my work even if people think my job is beneath them.

This is also where we begin to see work as a gift instead of a burden. I have a divine purpose. I also find proper pride in it. Not a curved-inward pride but a pride based on the honor of being God's coworker in his economy of love. Work is not a punishment; it is a gift. God works, and he honors us with work. If God works, then it is not beneath us but above us. So is rest. Rest is a gift too. God rested on the seventh day, and so should you—not on a particular day but in general. The Third Commandment, "Remember the Sabbath Day by keeping it holy" (Exod. 20:8) is no longer a rule we follow slavishly. We are free (Col. 2:16). Yet the principle remains. "Don't be workaholics," God seems to be saying to us. "Stop and enjoy this place. Trust me. The work will get done." It is a matter of trust. So the Sabbath command is to take time to be in contact with the means of grace. Take time to ponder what God has done for you. Go to church, receive his gifts, and enjoy all the gifts this world has to offer.

Ultimately this is pointing ahead to an eternal Sabbath rest (Heb. 4:9). When our work here on earth is done (six days), we will have a Sabbath (seventh day). The problem with this life is that there is always a Monday! We go through this seven-day work-Sabbath cycle over and over again until we arrive at the elusive eighth day of eternity. Yet this does not mean that we will be lazy in heaven, as if work ceased. I think of the eternal Sabbath rest as a sabbatical. The words are related. When someone takes a sabbatical, she does not spend six months lying on the couch. She works. But her work is free from the stresses of a regular job. She is afforded the time to explore or study a particular interest. She recharges not by napping on the couch but by working on something that will better herself and those around her. I imagine heaven as that kind of work. Good work. True flourishing and fulfilling work. God in his graciousness drops a bit of this heavenly shalom (flourishing) to us. There are days, even in the worst of jobs, when we get lost in the craft of our occupations. These are the days when it doesn't seem like we worked at all. We care nothing for a paycheck in those moments because we are so lost in the work itself. We once again lose ourselves in our vocations.

Gustaf Wingren speaks to this point when comparing the old man (sinner) to the new man (saint). The saint lives in a new kingdom, a realm of faith and love. Yet it is the same exact place the old man (the sinner) works and lives. "This is not really a new kingdom; as an 'old' man he has always lived in it, governed by law. Law, as it is embodied in the many offices, has the function, in the hand of God, to compel man to serve others, whether or not he wishes to do so. He operates his station, his vocation, by coercion, without his heart. But now, in faith and the gospel, the heart has been made new. Our neighbor with his need does not press upon us against our will; rather, he fills us with gladness, for it is our joy to serve him. What earthly government would compel, we now do freely. So love works on earth, in the realm of the law, yet it is not aware of any law. Heaven on earth. The boundary between heaven and earth has been bridged in this descent."[26]

Someday, when the struggle is over, we will be in our sabbatical rest. Until then, we plug along as sinner-saints, touched by heavenly shalom even in our vocations.

Freedom and Love

> Therefore notice this and differentiate between the free-
> dom existing in your relation to God and the freedom
> existing in your relation to your neighbor. In the former
> this freedom is present, in the latter it is not, and for this
> reason: God gives you this freedom only in the things
> that are yours, not in what is your neighbor's.
>
> —Martin Luther

Gene Edward Veith tells a story in his book *God at Work* about a struggling college student who studied hard and did all the things a good student should do. "Finally, exhausted, he realized he had to take a semester off. He took a job for the time being doing what he really enjoyed—namely, work-ing on cars. As an auto mechanic, he found himself rising in the ranks at the garage, taking on more responsibilities, and earning more and more money. He felt that he should go back to school, but he could not bring himself to quit his mechanic job. He was apologetic to his professor, but he should not have been. He had found his vocation."[27]

The young man also found freedom. He was free from pleasing God, his professors, and perhaps his parents and from the burden of the standard of success society placed upon his shoulders.

St. Paul writes that the Christian is dead to the law (Gal. 2:19). Remember that the Christian is simultaneously a sinner and a saint. The saint (the new man) is a slave to righteousness (Rom. 6:18). He cannot help but be righteous. He needs no law to tell him to do this or do that. He just does. He is free to be whom God made him to be, a lover of his neighbor. He sees a pile of dirty dishes and washes them. He performs this act of righteous love, often unaware at that moment that this deed was prepared in advance for him (Eph. 2:10). He is free. Free to love.

The old man, on the other hand, is under the law. He is a slave to sin (Rom. 6:20). He cannot help but sin. Even his outwardly good deeds are tainted by law. They are performed in the system of righteousness by law. He is bound to this system of law. At the end of life, when he takes stock of his time here on earth, he must wonder, "Was I good enough? Good enough to be blessed in the next world? Good enough to be remembered in favorable terms? Good enough to be at peace as I die?" The old man (sinner) is under the law and will continually put himself under the law. He knows no other system and cannot fathom freedom. As sinner-saints, Christians experience both types of emotions: the delights of freedom and the terrors of the law. As we already said, this spiritual battle is fought in the setting of vocation. Gustaf Wingren writes, "The Christian is both old and new man, not only in relation to God's judgment [and] God's forgiveness but also in his encounter with vocation and neighbor. He is still the old man, insofar as the encounter irritates him, and the new man when the encounter takes place with inner calm and joy."[28]

The old man looks at the neighbor and sees a thing. Something he uses for his own gain in the system of righteousness by law or an irritant that gets in his way. To the new man, the neighbor is a delight: "There is nothing more delightful and lovable on earth than one's neighbor."[29]

Wingren then summarizes Luther's view of programming spiritual growth and reform: "Luther [was] very modest about giving directions for reform of the world. He offers no program. . . . Love discovers for itself what is of the greatest benefit to a neighbor. It cannot busy itself with deeds prescribed by rules of propriety without ceasing to be love. It becomes a bondage under law, concern with one's own holiness, which, uncertain of salvation, seeks to achieve certainty by requiring sacrifice for a neighbor."[30] Care is to be taken by pastors not to place more law upon Christians who are free. Love knows no program. This is not to say that my feelings and desires, physical or emotional, should lead me to actions and/or relationships that are contrary to God's law. That is a curved-inward mind-set. This is not freedom but rather slavery to sinful desires. It is to say that true love is not bound by a set of man-made boundaries. Love flows to the neighbor. The neighbor's need dictates where love flows. There is no such thing as balance in life. Or, at least, it is not the goal we should set for ourselves at the outset. Balance happens, but only by serving the neighbor who needs us the most.

It isn't a matter of "balancing them" necessarily, as if they all demanded equal attention. Nor is it a matter of setting rigid priorities (as in, God first, family second, job third): since all vocations are about loving and serving one's neighbor, when vocations conflict, they should be resolved by attending to the neighbor with the greatest need.[31]

If we see our vocations as a conduit of God's love through us to our neighbor, then we are free from trying to balance life. It's God's love. It will flow where it needs to flow. If my job needs me, I am free to say no to my family. If my family needs me, I am free to say no to my job. This may mean searching for a new job or turning down a promotion because the demands of a new position would interfere with being a good parent, but that is OK too.[32] I do not need to worry about balance. This is God's responsibility.

But doesn't this all seem a little *cute*? This may work for upper-middle-class Americans living in a suburb whose greatest worry is whether or not their children are accepted into a good college or not. What about those living at the poverty line, let alone a subsistence farmer in a third world country? And isn't this all law anyway? If my whole life is geared toward the love of my neighbor, then it is all about me working. And quite frankly, what about me? What about my time? My joy? My vacation? My needs? My health?

There is no doubt that there are many talented musicians, math geniuses, and potential inventors who are subsistence farmers or migrant workers, or who find themselves in factories or cubicles where their talents are underused or even ignored. This is a sinful world in which people sin against their vocations, and the result is the opposite of human flourishing. It's tragic. But this does not mean that those workers are not valuable. They still do God's work, and it is important. Love may dictate that they work for their families and put aside their dreams. It is at once tragic and beautiful.[33] So is the cross.

We must never forget that for every vocation we find ourselves in, there are countless other vocations that serve us. I look around my office as I write this paragraph and I do not see four walls but construction workers, painters, electricians, truck drivers, architects, insurance agents, loan officers, administrators, masons, glassmakers, manufacturers, the inventor of the window air conditioner, the visionaries who started this college, the donors, deans, provosts, and on and on and on. And that's just so I can have an office. I simply cannot count the people whom God has used so that I can survive, let alone flourish. The love I give is not equal to the love I receive; it is not even close. So I am also free to see all the world as a gift. I can go out to eat, take in a ball game, go on vacation, and enjoy luxuries guilt-free. I am free. I have not been forgotten. It *is* about me because all these other vocations are God working for me.

This does not make me lazy but drives me all the more. It drives me to work for the flourishing of humanity—the way it was always supposed to be. It is a very small role I play, but it is important and the highest honor. I am a coworker with God.

Conclusion

Venture All Things

Thus a Christian man who lives in this confidence toward God knows all things, can do all things, ventures everything that needs to be done, and does everything gladly and willingly, not that he may gather merits and good works, but because it is a pleasure for him to please God in doing these things. He simply serves God with no thought of reward, content that his service pleases God.

—Martin Luther

Posture is important. So said our mothers and probably our pediatricians. Posture is important for our health (the pediatrician's concern) and our appearance and attitude (the mother's concerns). It also matters spiritually. Not physical posture but one's spiritual orientation. A curved-inward person's shoulders are slumped, and his chin touches his chest. He is inward-looking. He does not see what is in front of him. He thinks all the answers come from within himself, an inner light, belief in himself—all of the catchphrases from today's pop-psychologists. But what is within is rotten. The results can only be delusional pride or honest despair.

Now consider the person with good posture. Her shoulders are back, and her chin is up. She sees the world. She is even confident. God hammers us so that we will stop looking within. He lifts up our chin so we can see outside of ourselves. We look up, and we see Christ—specifically his cross. Here we see righteousness won for us and sins forgiven. Freedom! We look up, and we also become aware of our surroundings. We see our neighbor, perhaps for the very first time. There is Christ again. Vocation is a Christological endeavor. We see our role in the world. Purpose. We also look up and see the world as a gift. All this for us. All these vocations working for us. We see security and prosperity, albeit in a limited manner. Finally, we see flourishing. It's a brighter day.

Vocation is the setting for human flourishing. Shalom. The way it is supposed to be. Vocation is where God provides for his people. They need a certain level of prosperity, and he offers it through businessmen, investors, regulators, and entrepreneurs. They need a certain amount of security. He offers this too through governments, police, judges, and lawyers. They need purpose. Through vocation, humans are given a divine purpose. They need freedom. This too is protected through human means. But there is a greater freedom. A freedom from the damning law that terrorizes sinners. It all starts with Christ's justification of us through his life and death. His righteousness for our unrighteousness. This is true peace; this is true shalom. We are free. Free to flourish in love.

Yet the spiritual battle will continue to rage between the old man and the new man. Our old sinful natures turn gift into law and neighbor into nuisance. Our shoulders begin to slouch, and our chins drop. So God kills us again with his law. Damn that old man! Back to the waters of baptism for another death and resurrection. We do it all over again, but the burden is light. Christ takes us through it all again. Death and resurrection. Dying and living. "Look up!" he says to us again. "Look! Here I am. Here is your neighbor. Here is the world. I give it to you."

So we go back to work to fight the battle. Yet all along, God gets his work done. Vocation is the setting for his work. It's how he operates. What a privilege to be a part of it all. Even in the dark moments, Christ works with us. He's been through it all before and will take you through it all again. We are free from debilitating anxiety.

We possess supreme confidence in Christ. He has already overcome our greatest obstacles: sin and death. But we are more than survivors. He not only lifts us from the grave of despair but lifts us higher, to a grand and divine purpose. We are more than conquerors (Rom. 8:37). This world in which he has placed us is not a threat any longer. It is not a weight around our ankles. It is not a place from which we try to escape. This world is a gift. All of it. Work and rest. Joy and suffering. It is a gift given to free people. We possess, then, a supreme confidence. So much so that we are not driven by fear but rather can venture all things.

This "venturing all things" is only possible because of freedom. We are free to love. We do not take chances for ourselves; rather, we take chances in vocation. With sober enthusiasm, we are given good works to accomplish, planned in advance by God. We are free to do so because we are God's coworkers. We work and even take chances with him. We are curved outward in vocation. God makes sure of that. Venturing into this great unknown is only possible because our final destination is secure in Christ. There is no longer a fear of God's wrath. There is no longer even a desire to please him. That is taken care of at the cross. Nor do we carry the heavy burden of virtue for the sake of virtue. God uses us for the love of our neighbor. That's true virtue. The telos is not us but our neighbor. Nor do we carry the burden of searching for worthiness through man's opinion. We are at once not worthy of the call and underappreciated by the world, which cannot contemplate the sheer wonder that God works through us in our vocations. God justifies us. It's not our job; it's his. Here is where we find our value.

God doesn't have a plan for you; he has a plan for your neighbor. And it is quite an honor to be a vital part of this grand economy of love. And when all is said and done, we will realize that he had a plan for us too. It came through others, as God loves us through their vocations. The love we give is never the same as the love we receive. It's so much more.

A life of flourishing ends with a Solomon moment. After the great philosopher-king warned us about the meaningless of riches and even life itself, he had this to say: "This is what I have observed to be good: that it is appropriate for a person to eat, to drink and to find satisfaction in their toilsome labor under the sun during the few days of life God has given them—for this is their lot. Moreover, when God gives someone wealth and possessions, and the ability to enjoy them, to accept their lot and be happy in their toil—this is a gift of God. They seldom reflect on the days of their life, because God keeps them occupied with gladness of heart" (Eccl. 5:18–20). Not only is it permissible to enjoy a world of work and rest; it is God's desire for us. This may be our "lot in life," but in the freedom of Christ, it is also a gift. It is the gift of flourishing, the highest good: eudaimonia, happiness, shalom. So live free in the peace of Christ. Shalom, friends, shalom.

Epilogue 1

Vocation as the Setting for Evangelism

> Evangelism is the highest expression of priestly love for the neighbor as the confession of Christ calls the unbelieving neighbor out of the darkness of death into the life of the church. Speaking the words of God's law and gospel, the royal priesthood bears testimony to Christ Jesus in the places where God has put them: in their families, in the places of daily work, and with friends. It is within these contexts that the royal priesthood proclaims the praises of the Lord.
>
> —John Pless, "Reflections on the Life of the Royal Priesthood"

Evangelism is about relationships. Always has been, always will be. This is not to say that a local congregation should not go door to door, host events, have a robust online presence, and make use of all the other outreach techniques. They should. But it still comes down to the neighbor. And there is no greater gift to give to one's neighbor than the peace of

Christ. Since vocation is all about the neighbor, vocation is the setting for evangelism. It may seem that the elevation of vocation will result in the devaluation of evangelism efforts, but this is a misguided conclusion. The family, community, and occupations of a Christian are not at war with the local congregation fighting for the precious minutes and dollars of the individual. The truth is that vocation is where neighbors are engaged in a meaningful way.

Vocation is the setting where meaningful relationships are formed and trust is earned. Whether it be in the family or at work, vocation is the place where Christians have the most contact with non-Christians. Christians are not *of* the world, but they are *in* the world. You may not know everything about your coworkers, but you spend a lot of time with them. These are your neighbors. It will not go unnoticed if you perceive your job as a calling. You might even be labeled as the coworker who "has it all together" (even if you don't).

St. Paul calls this the ambition for a quiet life. He writes to the persecuted Thessalonian Christians, "Make it your ambition to lead a quiet life: You should mind your own business and work with your hands, just as we told you, so that your daily life may win the respect of outsiders and so that you will not be dependent on anybody" (1 Thess. 4:11–12).

How can one be ambitious about a quiet life? The Greek word translated "ambition" is actually two words put together: *love* and *honor*. To love honor is to have an ambition, to consider something an honor, or to aspire toward a goal. For the Thessalonian Christians, it was to avoid idleness, to perform their jobs; in short, it was to fulfill their vocations until Christ's return. Nothing has changed. The Christian ambition is to see one's life's work as an honor. This sets Christians apart in a unique manner. Don't be surprised if people notice. You may be trusted. People may even look up to you. A sense of vocation makes you a better worker, more diligent, kinder, and calmer. And yet real.

Totally aware of the difficulties of your particular job and sympathetic to the coworker who complains about the boss, the vendors, or the customers. You might just be the person your fellow coworker seeks out for advice, even spiritual advice.

These meaningful relationships often turn into meaningful conversations. Vocation is the setting where we have meaningful conversations and, therefore, where deep thoughts of life, death, sin, and grace take place. The cordial relationship you have with an in-law or a coworker may take the next step when you find yourself at an office party, at a family gathering, or out for a drink after the workday. The facade is lifted, and you are forced to get to know the person. Who is he? How does he think? What are his goals, his struggles? What does he think about the big questions in life? It happens. It happens because of vocation.

Vocation is also the setting where people suffer and, therefore, the place where the gospel can be preached. Those relationships and those conversations inevitably touch upon the tragic nature of our world and of our lives. Eventually, you will find out what bothers them, what hurts them, and what haunts them. If you are the authentic coworker who is trusted, who has opened up, and who has listened, an opportunity for gospel preaching may just present itself. Perhaps more often than we think. Vocation is the setting for evangelism.

Epilogue 2

Choosing a Vocation

This is also why it is wrong to treat God as a grand employment agency, a celestial executive searcher to find perfect fits for our perfect gifts. The truth is not that God is finding us a place for our gifts but that God has created us and our gifts for a place of his choosing—and we will only be ourselves when we are finally there.

—Os Guinness, *The Call*

This might sound counterintuitive coming from a college professor whose job depends on convincing students to spend a lot of money in exchange for an education from a liberal arts university, but you don't have to go to college. You don't. Competition for students is fierce. It actually drives up costs (better dorms, better food, etc.). Tuition is insane. Don't get me wrong; a liberal arts education is priceless. But this is a competition, and so college administrators are forced to sell their product. Some will make the case that a graduate from a four-year institution will earn, on average, more than a high school graduate, far exceeding the cost of college tuition. Eventually. Maybe. It depends on what job you land, right? Not everybody is buying the sales pitch. If a high schooler can learn a trade and start earning (and saving) at eighteen without the debt of college, he or she will be better off in the long run. Maybe. So worried mothers and fathers wonder, "What should my child do?"

Although financial concerns are real, perhaps we are asking the wrong question. I have often been asked by such parents for advice on this very dilemma. Recently I have begun to answer the inquiry with my own questions: "What kind of high school did your son attend? Did he learn history? Was he forced to engage in literature? What electives did he take?" We need thoughtful mechanics, carpenters, caretakers, and civil servants as much as we need thoughtful doctors, lawyers, and teachers for the flourishing of our society. And yet education is more than all that—more than money, more than an informed electorate. It is about freedom once again. It's in the name, liberal arts. The free arts as opposed to the servile arts. Both are good and honorable but historically, the former was for free people, the latter for servants. Servants were not afforded the leisure to study subjects or hone skills that were unnecessary for them to perform their jobs. Their education could include engineering or language skills, but its purpose was to serve a higher class of society.

This is, of course, still true in many places around the world. For many, the idea of career choice is laughable. But for those of us who have been afforded the opportunity to think, study, write, and read, we are blessed. We have been given a gift. We have been afforded the kind of freedom most people in the history of the world could have only dreamed of. Those who see education as only a means to make money are what Aristotle called the "most vulgar."[1]

Both the argument that an expensive liberal arts education will make the individual more money and the argument for the trades making more financial sense are incomplete. So what high school did you go to? If you received a fine education in the arts, the free arts, so that you can think clearly and widely, and if you have a calling to an occupation that does not require an advanced degree, then go! It will be beautiful and meaningful if you are driven to continue your education. You are free to do so. Go! Forget about the money for a second and just work hard.

Still, the question haunts many of you, I am sure: "How do I know what to do?" The tyranny of choice is the curse of an affluent society. There are too many options. We make it worse by asking our children from kindergarten on what they *want* to be when they grow up. How are they supposed to know at that age or any age? And so the pressure of a looming decision mounts throughout the years. Your whole life and financial future riding on this one decision! This hardly seems like a calling. In fact, if you are waiting for a voice in your head to tell you what to do, you will be waiting a long time (or be driven mad).[2]

Life is full of these kinds of choices. Should I go to college? Which school? Should I stay at my job or find another? Focus on my family or career? For those who are thinking about these tough choices, please know that God will narrow it down for you. He will make the choice for you. You won't know it until years later, maybe not until heaven, but he will make the choice for you. He will call you. Until then, the choice is yours; at least, that is how we should look at it. It's our responsibility. So how do we know what to choose? Here are some things to think about.

Stop asking yourself what you want, and start asking yourself what gifts you have been blessed with. Don't worry; God has a plan for you too; you are the neighbor in a myriad of plans in which God uses others in their vocations to serve you. The love you give will always be less than the love you receive. It's the difference between being curved inward ("What do I want?") and curved outward ("What gifts have I been given for the love of my neighbor?").

Vocation is always in the here and now. What's in front of you right now? If it is family, then let it be family. If it is a minimum-wage job for right now, then be the best worker at that task there ever has been. If the scholarship money is enough to make college affordable, then go for it. If you need a job and one in your field is not available, that's OK. Vocation is in the here and now. What's in front of you right now? The right here and the right now will change, but it's God's job to change it, not yours.

God almost exclusively uses the ordinary to accomplish the extraordinary. So he is not going to call you as he did Samuel in the middle of the night (1 Sam. 3). But he has given you parents, counselors, teachers, coaches, and friends to give you advice. Listen to all of them.

I know that you want to make a difference, but don't let that blind you to what God has in store for you. Whatever you do, it will make a difference. All labor matters, and "all labor has dignity."[3]

I don't know where you will be five years from now or ten years from now; neither do you. But I do know that God has prepared good works in advance for you (Eph. 2:10). He knows that some of you will be at the beds of the dying, giving comfort to the patients and their families alike. He knows that some of you will be at a board meeting making decisions with serious ramifications for communities and economies. He knows that some of you will be building bridges, paving roads, driving school buses, balancing checkbooks, changing diapers, coaching Little League, tutoring schoolchildren, or writing laws. You don't know what is in your future, but he knows. He is preparing you for those moments. He is preparing you for the neighbor who will soon be in front of you. So with sober enthusiasm, venture all things.

Nurse

Do you know what it takes to be a nurse? The amount of information they have to learn is beyond what I could memorize. And it's not the type of information that can be a little bit off. Nursing mistakes cost lives. It's a lot of pressure. But what a great feeling to help the sick, to comfort the infirm, to be present at births, or to see modern medicine work its miracles. It's not always easy to be a nurse, but it is good work.

Road Construction Worker

Can you imagine working on a freeway? It must be rewarding to drive on the road *you* built. It's complicated stuff. There is engineering involved, as well as a lot of math and intricate machinery. And yet it is not a desk job; it is physically demanding. Oh, and all this with cars whizzing by you at seventy miles per hour. It's not always easy to be a road construction worker, but it is good work.

Chef

Nobody has more going on at once than a chef. It's not for everybody. Do not get in the way of a chef when the kitchen gets busy. Everything has to run smoothly and on time. But the creations that are made! Food is one of the greatest joys of our world. And you get to be the creator. It's not always easy to be a chef, but it is good work.

Electrical Line Worker

Have you ever seen the men hanging from helicopters, working on electrical lines? Danger doesn't begin to describe it. All so I can turn on my TV and keep my food cold. I would imagine the electrical line worker thinking about how important his job is as he looks across the horizon and sees not trees and fields but miles and miles of powerlines. If he messes up at his job, a lot of people are going to have bad days. It's not always easy to be an electrical line worker, but it is good work.

Factory Worker

Many jobs carry with them particular crosses. Teachers deal with irrational parents. Farmers always seem to be battling against the forces of nature and the market. Yet there might not be a heavier burden than the tedium and often difficult job of a factory worker. And yet it is in the name, *factory*—they make something. They can point to a car on the road, to a packaged item at the store, and say, "I made that." It's not always easy to be a factory worker, but it is good work.

Lawyer

It is easy to hate lawyers, but we need them. At its core, the law desires truth and peace in a sinful world. In a fallen world, the law acts as a curb so that we do not fly into chaos and anarchy. Lawyers navigate this messy world. At their best, they are champions of truth and fairness facing insurmountable odds (a sinful world). It's not always easy to be a lawyer, but it is good work.

Truck Driver

Driving a truck takes some serious skill. Can you back up a trailer? It's not easy. There is a lot at stake too. There are often thousands of dollars of merchandise these guys are hauling atop a huge missile full of diesel traveling seventy miles per hour down a highway. Lives are at stake. And don't think the driver doesn't think about exactly that. In heavy traffic, they are often only inches away from other vehicles. One mistake and all is lost. But the open road! They get to see the whole country from mountains to plains, from shores to big cities. They keep the country's economy rolling. It's not always easy to be a truck driver, but it is good work.

Notes

Introduction

1 This does not mean that non-Christian work is not good, valuable, or used by God. Quite the opposite. The terminology is just different. A non-Christian is in a station (e.g., doctor), but the Christian's station has an added dimension (a call from God). An atheist doctor would not consider himself "called by God," but a Christian lawyer can and should.

2 The gospel is the good news that God does not count a human's sin against him or her on account of Christ's perfect life and innocent death.

3 The Christian is simultaneously a sinner and a saint. The sinful nature (or old man) is 100 percent sinner. The new creation in Christ is 100 percent saint. The sinner cannot help but sin. The saint (or new creation) cannot produce anything but righteousness.

4 LW 31:344. All citations from the works of Martin Luther (unless indicated otherwise) will be abbreviated as LW and are taken from *Luther's Works*, 55 vols., ed. Jaroslav Pelikan and Helmut T. Lehman (Philadelphia: Fortress, 1955–86).

Chapter 1

1 In this culture, only sons typically possessed the legal right to an inheritance. By calling all Christians "sons," Paul stated that both male and female were treated equally in grace.

2 Then again, if it is God's love through us, it is unlimited.

3 What would our case look like? I suppose we would blame our par-
    ents, society, or the government. That tactic didn't work in elemen-
    tary school; it's not going to work before God.

4 The full quote reads, "Facientibus quod in se est, Deus non den-
    egat gratiam." It means "To those who do what is in them, God will
    not deny grace." Richard A. Mueller, *Dictionary of Latin and Greek
    Theological Terms* (Grand Rapids, MI: Baker Books, 1985), 13.

5 Gustaf Wingren, *Luther on Vocation*, trans. Carl C. Rasmussen
    (Eugene, OR: Wipf and Stock, 1957), 10.

6 If we need to add something to our salvation, then Christ's death was
    not good enough (Gal. 2:21). How would this be to his glory?

7 Martin Luther, "Small Catechism," in *The Book of Concord: The
    Confessions of the Evangelical Lutheran Church*, ed. Robert Kolb
    and Timothy Wengert (Minneapolis: Fortress, 2000), 365 (emphasis
    mine).

8 Aidan Nichols, *Looking at the Liturgy* (San Francisco: Ignatius Press,
    1996), 97.

9 Nichols, 97.

10 Os Guinness, *The Call* (Nashville: Thomas Nelson, 1998), 27–42.

11 Guinness, 39.

12 Dorothy Sayers, "Why Work?," TNL, accessed February 13, 2016,
    http://tnl.org/wpcontent/uploads/Why-Work-Dorothy-Sayers.pdf.

13 LW 45:40.

Chapter 2

1 LW 31:53.

Chapter 3

1 You did what is in you! Medieval Christianity all over again.

2 God the Father does this for him. He demands perfection from sin-
    ners and faith from dead hearts. This is law. God then provides what
    he demands in Christ. This is gospel.

3 LW 31:344. See 1 Corinthians 9:19.

4 Wingren, *Luther on Vocation*, 13.

5 Wingren, 12.

6 LW 46:126.

7 Wingren, *Luther on Vocation*, 6.

8 "One human being may not take the life of another; but God is free
   and does so. He does it through the offices of judge and executioner.
   To the judge God says, 'If you do not kill and punish, you shall be
   punished'; for then the judge would fail his vocation. Man must not
   look on a woman to lust after her; but in the 'station' which God
   instituted for the propagation of the race, God himself effects desire
   thereby. A minister must not condemn anyone; but the office of
   preaching does so." Wingren, *Luther on Vocation*, 7.

9 LW 46:96.

10 For the record, I really like teaching freshmen. It is a delight to open
   Scripture up to them.

11 It is always dangerous to start too many sentences with "I am." Those
   two words are reserved for someone higher. See Exodus 3:14 and
   John 6:35–51, 8:12, 10:7–14, 11:25, 14:6, and 15:1–5.

12 Daniel Deutschlander, *The Theology of the Cross: Reflections on His
   Cross and Ours* (Milwaukee, WI: Northwestern Publishing House,
   2008), 36–37.

13 "Vocation counters the materialism and self-centeredness of economic pursuits by giving them a new meaning and a new orientation. Similarly, vocation also transforms other social relationships,
   such as the nature of authority. . . . [It] is not a matter of exercising
   power over them. Rather, authority must be used in love and service to those under authority." Gene Edward Veith, *Working for Our
   Neighbor: A Lutheran Primer on Vocation, Economics, and Ordinary
   Life* (Grand Rapids, MI: Christian's Library Press, 2016), 17.

14 Wingren, *Luther on Vocation*, 8 (emphasis in original).

15 David Brooks, *The Road to Character* (New York: Random House,
   2015), 91–92.

16 Schweitzer, quoted in Brooks, 92.

17 Wingren, *Luther on Vocation*, 181–82.

18 Wingren, 233.

19 John Douglas Hall, *Lighten Our Darkness: Towards an Indigenous
   Theology of the Cross* (Lima, OH: Academic Renewal Press, 2001),
   117.

Chapter 4

1 The truth is that many of us are just as happy in the present as we
   were in the past and will be in the future. Usually we are so happy

that we do not have time to ask ourselves if we are happy or not happy.

2 Anthony M. Kennedy, "A Dialogue on Freedom, Included in the National Conference of Citizenship: Conference Report," September 19, 2005 (Washington, DC, 2005), 36, accessed September 22, 2015, http://www.civicenterprises.net/MediaLibrary/Docs/national_conference_on_citizenship_2005.pdf.

3 "What is always chosen as an end in itself and never as a means to something else is called final in an unqualified sense. This description seems to apply to happiness above all else: for we always choose happiness as an end in itself and never for the sake of something else. Honor pleasure, intelligence, and all virtue we choose partly for themselves—for we would choose each of them even if no further advantage would accrue from them—but we also choose them partly for the sake of happiness, because we assume that it is through them that we will be happy. On the other hand, no one chooses happiness for the sake of honor, pleasure, and the like, nor as a means to anything at all." Aristotle, *Nicomachean Ethics*, trans. Martin Ostwald (Indianapolis: Hackett, 1961), 1097a35–1097b6.

4 Cornelius Plantinga, *Not the Way It's Supposed to Be: A Breviary of Sin* (Grand Rapids, MI: Eerdmans, 1995), 10.

5 Aristotle, *Nicomachean Ethics* 1095b14–16.

6 Bryan Dik and Ryan Duffy, *Make Your Job a Calling: How the Psychology of Vocation Can Change Your Life at Work* (West Conshohocken, PA: Templeton Press, 2012), 9.

7 Dik and Duffy, 9.

8 Dik and Duffy, 16.

9 Dik and Duffy, 17.

10 Dik and Duffy, 4.

11 *Catechism of the Catholic Church* (New York: Doubleday, 1995) 564.

12 Think of the words we use for conception and birth. Do we *procreate*, or do we *reproduce*? Are our children creations (procreate) or are they matter that we produce from our matter (reproduce)? Humans created in the image of God are the types of beings who create!

13 Gene Edward Veith, *The Spirituality of the Cross* (St. Louis: Concordia Publishing House, 1999), 71–72.

14 When this happens, it is the result of God using other people, such as your boss, in their vocations/stations to love you.

15 Wingren, *Luther on Vocation*, 45.

16 Matthew B. Crawford, *Shop Class as Soulcraft: An Inquiry into the Value of Work* (New York: Penguin, 2010), 24.

17 Crawford, *Shop Class as Soulcraft*, 5.

18 Crawford, 37–38.

19 Crawford, 19.

20 Crawford, 127.

21 Crawford, 128.

22 Crawford, 157.

23 Crawford, 158.

24 Crawford, 157.

25 Crawford, 181.

26 Wingren, *Luther on Vocation*, 47.

27 Gene Edward Veith, *God at Work: Your Christian Calling in All of Life* (Wheaton, IL: Crossway Books, 2002), 53.

28 Wingren, *Luther on Vocation*, 55.

29 Wingren, 43.

30 Wingren, 48–49.

31 Gene Edward Veith and Mary J. Moerbe, *Family Vocation: God's Calling in Marriage, Parenting, and Childhood* (Wheaton, IL: Crossway Books, 2012), 228.

32 I am not saying that family and work are necessarily equal. Family has to come first in the sense that as a parent, for example, there is a duty that is unique to the father and mother. Nobody can fill this office the same way. To be sure, certain vocations are unique and will take precedence, but this is because of the unique relationship with the neighbor involved.

33 We should note that the tragic nature of poverty is often because of people sinning against their vocations (e.g., a corrupt governmental official or a greedy businessman). The answer is a proper understanding of one's neighbor and vocation.

Epilogue 2

1 Aristotle, *Nicomachean Ethics* 1095b14–16.

2 And of course, if God told us what to do, we would complain about our lack of freedom—like Jonah!

3 Martin Luther King Jr., *All Labor Has Dignity* (Boston: Beacon Press, 2011), 172.